THE POWER OF CONFLICT

Also by Jon Taffer

Don't Bullsh*t Yourself!

Raise the Bar

THE POWER OF CONFLICT

SPEAK YOUR MIND AND GET THE RESULTS YOU WANT

JON TAFFER

WILLIAM MORROW

An Imprint of HarperCollinsPublishers

Author's Note: Where only single names are used, with the exception of television episodes, all identifying details have been changed to protect the innocent. In some cases, composite characters have been created.

THE POWER OF CONFLICT. Copyright © 2022 by Jon Taffer. All rights reserved. Printed in the United States of America. No part of this book may be used or reproduced in any manner whatsoever without written permission except in the case of brief quotations embodied in critical articles and reviews. For information, address HarperCollins Publishers, 195 Broadway, New York, NY 10007.

HarperCollins books may be purchased for educational, business, or sales promotional use. For information, please email the Special Markets Department at SPsales@harpercollins.com.

A hardcover edition of this book was published in 2022 by William Morrow, an imprint of HarperCollins Publishers.

FIRST PAPERBACK EDITION PUBLISHED 2023.

Designed by Kyle O'Brien

Library of Congress Cataloging-in-Publication Data has been applied for.

ISBN 978-0-06-314110-0

23 24 25 26 27 LBC 5 4 3 2 1

To my grandson Rhett: I hope you always stand up for yourself and those things that are important to you.

CONTENTS

THE POWER OF CONFLICT

INTRODUCTION

If you have ever seen me on *Bar Rescue* or *Marriage Rescue,* my hit reality shows about saving failing bars and troubled marriages, you could be forgiven for thinking that I am just a naturally in-your-face kind of guy. You probably noticed that there is always at least one moment in an episode where I get into someone's space and start yelling. I am big, loud, and intense—a physically imposing and intimidating presence—so most would assume that being combative is my go-to reflex. But they would be wrong. In fact, I am almost always calculating about how and when I go there. The passion is real because I care deeply about helping these people, but the emotion is underpinned with a kind of science. I leverage these verbal explosions to move the needle in the direction I want it to go. And they work, every time.

I've used the power of conflict instinctively for years. But it wasn't until recently, as I was watching dozens of brave souls stand up for their beliefs in a challenging political and social climate, that it struck me just how necessary conflict is for a free and healthy society, and how fundamental my unique approach to confrontation has been to my overall success.

My first book, *Raise the Bar: An Action-Based Method for Maximum Customer Reactions,* taught business owners how to create and control the reactions of their customers to gain a business advantage. My second book, *Don't Bullsh*t Yourself!: Crush the Excuses That Are*

Holding You Back, gave general readers some bare-knuckled methods for being honest with themselves and pushing past the blind spots toward positive action. Both books touched on aspects of conflict, including engaging with others and being honest with yourself. But they didn't tell the whole story. They didn't spell out the profoundly positive impact of conflict when you are willing to step into the arena and fight the good fight for what you know in your heart to be right. Everything I have done in my life and career has led me to the understanding that conflict is not only a good thing, it's *transformational*.

This book is the result of that epiphany, and the place where I codify my signature Taffer Toolkit for Constructive Conflict. There is a smart, effective way to deal with any kind of confrontation. When a dispute arises or is provoked, there is a method that will enable you to manipulate the situation to get the results that you want. On these next pages, I will show you how, through a multitude of real-life circumstances from my own life and career, as well as anecdotes from others who mustered the courage to engage in conflict and make their case for the betterment of their own lives, and the lives of others. Of course, conflict is something that you use selectively and strategically. This is about the conscious, nonemotional practice of conflict, complete with rules of engagement to achieve a goal or fulfill an underlying purpose.

I feel a deep sense of urgency as I make this case for conflict and the constructive ways to engage in the chapters that follow. Never has the timing and content of a book I'm authoring mattered more to me. We can no longer hide from the fight, because the world as we know it needs, and deserves, defending. For the sake of our children, our communities, and our country, we must be willing to enter the fray. The fight has finally come to us, and retreating is not an option. I am challenging you to speak your mind, because the time to start working on your conflict skills is now!

Why did we ever stop speaking up? Why did we stop defending and debating our ideals? And when did we become so conflict-avoidant that we can't even talk about the values that mean everything to us at the dinner table with our own families?

Sometimes we are too darn quiet. Our tendency to hold back has created a void that is filled by others who then drown out all that defines who we are. If we don't speak up and allow our voices to be heard, no minds will be changed and all that matters will be hijacked by the noisy minority, because silence no longer wins the day.

I understand why many of you may wish to run from the fight. When you suddenly find yourself on the "wrong" side of popular opinion, even when you are speaking the truth, it can be isolating and terrifying. Staying in line seems like the safer option, at least in the short term. But the necessity of defending your values, your livelihood, and even your life against the mob has never been greater.

In my role as a restaurateur and bar owner representing thousands of small businesses across America, I've seen how corrupt individuals at the local and state government level, under the cover of COVID and emergency executive power, have made power grabs, singling out and punishing individuals who've tried to keep their businesses running, the lights on, and food on the tables for their children and their employees' children.

We cannot be afraid to do battle for a righteous cause. If that means coming into conflict with others, so be it. Bring it on! Because the time has come to speak up with class, conviction, and grace. By no means am I suggesting that voicing our beliefs involves being a jerk on social media or engaging in personal or physical attacks. We are not in the business of destruction, and stealing individual dignity from one another does not accomplish our goals. Instead, I am talking about sticking up for what we believe in, in an honorable way. But that does not necessarily mean you should be soft or understated in the engagement. The time has come to turn up the volume!

So are you going to continue to watch silently, swallowing your principles as your disappointment in the way life is going eats away at your soul? Or will you join me on these next pages as we build up our conflict muscles to righteously step up and speak out?

You don't have to go full tilt as I've been known to do on my show. Sometimes the right decision is to *not* engage when you don't find a worthy opponent. Sometimes all it takes to speak your conscience is a calm, even tone bolstered by a set of irrefutable facts. There is a method to match any battle you may be facing.

In the following chapters, I will lay out my approach for mastering a strategic response to conflict—how to *act* affirmatively rather than *react* disproportionately. To leverage conflict deliberately, constructively, and productively, I argue that you need to assess the situation before acting upon it. Expect an array of strategies, as well as more granular techniques, like looking into the eyes of the person on the other side of the confrontation for the dilation of pupils, a telltale sign for exactly when to step into their space to land your point. Or when to say something encouraging or conciliatory, with a hand gently pressing on the shoulder, so that the person on the other side of the conflict will be taken off guard and more inclined to listen. I promise, you don't have to be a cigar-chomping loudmouth like me to be effective at conflict. These tools are accessible to anyone!

My aim is to build up your confidence step-by-step, so that boldly fighting for your principles will always be an option when that moment comes for you to face down the mob of one, or a thousand. So the next time someone tries to block, demean, or dismiss you, think about the stakes. But first, study the methods I will share with you on these next pages to make your case, hold your ground, and get the results you want. Because what you stand for matters. Your principles are always worth the fight.

1

THE CASE FOR CONFLICT

Why constructive engagement is good for you.

One of the most explosive confrontations I experienced in my career happened while taping the third episode of the first season of my show *Bar Rescue*, and it came out of nowhere. The declining bar in question was an Irish pub called the Abbey, in Chicago. During a key moment on camera where I introduced myself to the entire bar staff and owner, offering them advice and letting them know what the stakes were if they failed to improve their performance, an executive of the network I'd never before met decided to insert himself.

This gentleman, whom we'll call "Joe," stepped right in front of me, stopped the cameras, and started giving direction to the Abbey's crew.

"You, over there, I want you to look angry," he told one of the bartenders who had the misfortune to make eye contact with him. "And *you*, you're boring me! Start reacting. I wanna see tears!" he shouted at a waitress, insulting the poor woman to make her cry.

As I watched this aggressive and uncalled-for interference unfold, I could feel my temperature rising, so I removed myself from the scene to quietly process what was happening and formulate an appropriate response. I walked out of the bar and across the street to the building where the crew and monitors were, with Joe following close behind me. I said nothing as he continued talking, throwing out orders at me, one of which was the suggestion that I take a tampon, cover it in ketchup, and plant it on the bathroom floor of the bar.

By then I'd had enough, so I spun around to face him.

"Are you telling me to be a liar on camera?"

"Jon, I'm just telling you how to make it a better show."

"Oh really? And is that why you interrupted and undermined me in front of people who need to respect me if they're going to heed my advice for the rest of filming? What kind of an idiot does that?"

Now, I was a newbie to the world of reality show production. We had a crew of fifty people running around, showrunners, producers . . . a lot of folks who knew more than I did. I was in awe of the process, and excited by the prospect of filming my first ten-episode season. But the one thing I told the producers from the beginning was that we had to be authentic. I knew other reality shows were scripted, but I wasn't impressed by that fact. This was about me maintaining my values rather than working for the network. Others might be okay with flipping over tables and manufacturing arguments for the sake of being on TV, but I'd already made my money. I was in this to educate bar owners and hopefully make an entertaining TV show, not sell myself out or humiliate the folks I was there to help.

The exchange with Joe was getting heated. He was rude and disruptive, coming at me like a tough guy hell-bent on imposing his will. But I was not having it. I persisted in challenging him until it was clear we were getting nowhere. This man had no integrity and was not worth my time. In that moment, I made the conscious choice to risk it all.

"Your mind isn't right. You don't think about things correctly. Go fuck yourself!"

I threw Joe off the set, and he spent the next six hours sitting and, by all accounts, sulking inside a McDonald's a block away while we shut down filming. The next morning a group of senior executives flew in from Los Angeles to talk me off the ledge. They knew I was prepared to walk away, and they had a show to save.

"Jon, you can have creative disagreements with us, you can be angry with us, but you cannot tell an executive to go fuck himself!" the executive vice president told me.

But he realized I meant what I said, and that I was prepared to shut the show down. I might have been a young punk to television, but everyone from the gaffer to the sound guy was clear on where I stood. This wasn't just about the quality of the show. It was about my integrity. We resumed shooting and the subject was dropped. From that day on, I was never asked to film anything that wasn't truthful, and Joe never again appeared on my set (nor did he last at the network for long).

Your Values Matter

I don't care who you are, where you come from, or what you do. There will *always* be moments in life where you must be prepared to face conflict. As long as you are living and breathing, there will come a point when you must stand up for yourself and what you believe in. You matter. Your values and opinions matter. Knowing this, how dare you stay silent in the face of a challenge? How dare you allow yourself to be bullied into disavowing your principles by anyone, be it a business adversary, a spouse, an employer, a family member, or a bunch of angry strangers on social media?

In a society as free as ours supposedly is, where we have been blessed with a depth of choices, we have an obligation to stand by the decisions we make or the identity we choose. Whether you are a young LGBTQ person or a born-again Christian, a Democrat or a Republican, a baseball player who kneels for the national anthem or a basketball player who stands, the day must come when you are prepared to step into the ring and fight for who you are and the things you care about, your Facebook "friends" be damned!

Yeah, that's right, I said it. We live in an era where any dissent from the prevailing orthodoxy of political groups or movements, on either side, can get people fired, doxed, or deplatformed. Speaking up can result in maligned reputations, families and lives threatened or destroyed. That's why, for many, conflict is scary. It leaves them frozen in fear, deflecting and even *apologizing* to avoid having to engage in vigorous debate. They would rather stay part of the silent majority, watching in quiet horror as all they hold dear gets eviscerated by a noisy few.

And how is that working out for you? The less often people take a stand, the more the mob rules. When you keep sitting there and taking all the abuse, you diminish yourself. You're not living your life fully, and you're giving away precious little pieces of your soul. But it's never enough for the bullies. The more you back down and apologize, refusing to engage in confrontation, the less they'll be satisfied and the more they will demand. Worst of all, you'll be letting yourself down.

I get it. The thought of conflict stirs in most of us, well, conflicting emotions. It can lead to disagreements that destroy friendships, make office politics unbearable, and, in the extreme, trigger riots, war, and bloodshed. You might be thinking, *Wait a minute. Isn't the goal of civilization to reduce or eliminate conflict? War is bad. Strife between peoples is bad.* Not necessarily. Would Hitler have been stopped? Would the Civil Rights Act have passed? On a personal level, would your kid finally have stood up to the schoolyard bully and ended the daily torment by fighting back? No, no, and no.

Without conflict, none of us stands for anything. But what we can gain when we are willing to engage in positive conflict is immense. I risked everything in that moment with Joe the TV executive. But we probably would not have made it to eight seasons and more than two hundred episodes of *Bar Rescue* had I not engaged in that conflict.

Today, we have rewritten the rules of reality television. Many of the fans among our more than 118 million unique viewers (at the time of writing) have said they love our show precisely because we are authentic and unscripted. We've inspired millions of small business owners to take back their lives and their businesses, and I've been blessed with a media platform that allows me to continue to inspire millions more. All because I was willing to go toe-to-toe with the network and battle for my right to uphold my values and keep it real.

Forcing the Issue

I've lost count of the number of inflection points in my life where my willingness to engage in constructive conflict has raised me to the next level. Although I wasn't always in control of the circumstances and timing, once put in that situation, I was deliberate in my response to it. I guarantee that moment will inevitably come, because taking risks in business and in life is *never* without conflict. I repeat, that's a *good* thing. The conflicts that come up between employer and employees, for example, can produce great outcomes if handled well.

There are moments when, in order to resolve a toxic problem, you may even have to force a conflict, like I did during a Season Three episode of *Bar Rescue* called "Hostile Takeover" in which three bar owners constantly argued with each other about numerous trivialities instead of focusing on the root cause of the bar's business problems.

One partner, Jerry, held a 40 percent interest in the bar. He was also a drinker. The other two partners each held a 30 percent interest. Because they mistakenly believed that Jerry was the majority stakeholder, and because they were so uncomfortable with the idea of addressing Jerry's drinking problem, nothing was getting done and the useless bickering continued. Until I came along. I told the two minority stakeholders that together they were actually majority owners. That gave them power and confidence. It took some doing, but I was able to get them to address Jerry's problem together, escort him out of the bar and the business, and get back to what was important—running a profitable bar. Once they understood their combined majority stake, they were able to harness their power together and resolve the elephant-in-the-room conflict: Jerry and his drinking.

That episode illustrates one of the many positives that constructive conflict can bring to your most important relationships. Doing battle for a worthy or righteous cause can evoke emotional ties we have to those family, friends, and allies with whom we have faced adversity together. Confronting conflict with allies strengthens the bonds of family, friends, and colleagues. By acknowledging those feelings, we're also recognizing that facing conflict gives us the chance to build even stronger relationships. (And Jerry, now sober, has since become a dear friend who reaches out to me every holiday.)

Conversely, unresolved conflict can become so toxic that it destroys relationships. It also stifles growth and forces individuals to retreat from engagement in any worthy pursuit. Consider what it must be like for the astronauts and cosmonauts orbiting Earth and living in confined spaces with each other for months on end. Imagine how those tiny annoyances can fester inside a space station where there's no escape from the people whose habits, actions, and insensitivities are driving you crazy.

Cosmonaut Valentine Lebedev didn't have to imagine. In 1982

he lived it for 211 days on Russia's Salyut 7 space station, and wrote about it in his memoir, *Diary of a Cosmonaut.*[1] It's not as if he could go outside to walk off any tensions or get some air. After a while, the stress became unbearable.

"We don't understand what's going on with us. We silently walk by each other, feeling offended. We have to find some way to make things better."[2]

The cosmonaut's space stint with fellow traveler Alexander "Tolia" Ivanchenkov, along with the various scientists, doctors, engineers, and backup cosmonauts who flew to the station for shorter stints, consisted of maintaining sanity amid the monotony, proximity, and discomforts of living 140 miles above the Earth without family, fresh air, the comforts of home, and, well, gravity. Some diary entries detail the stress of equipment failures and the hours spent in tense silence trying to make repairs. Inside a space not much bigger than a mobile home, strewn with cables, papers, and various space station debris that was not nailed down, they lived and toiled, aware that everything they did, no matter how routine it might have seemed on Earth, from planting cucumber seeds in their space garden to cleaning out the human waste to keep their plumbing system functioning, necessitated meticulous attention to detail. Sometimes the level of irritation with the circumstances, and each other, could be so high that the two men would not utter a word to each other for days at a time.

"And what's the problem?" Lebedev asks himself on day 115 of orbiting space. "Am I prejudiced against my crewman, or am I just that kind of person? No, it's just a fact of life which we are always afraid to admit to without sweetening, smoothing the sharp edges, assuming that someone might misunderstand us or misinterpret us."[3]

Lebedev breaks down his difficult and complicated relationship with Ivanchenkov, which veers between affection and exasperation.

"We cosmonauts prepare and train ourselves inside the same

team for years. It's tiring. . . . We have to find enough strength within ourselves (which isn't so easy) to build open and trusting relationships within the team, form a consensus on our work, and prepare for the difficulties of flight. The most important thing in the relationship between Tolia and me is the acceptance and recognition of the strong and weak points in each other's personalities. On top of that we mustn't forget to spare each other's vanity, protect each other and actually be friends instead of pretending . . ."[4]

Astronaut's Oath

In the end, Lebedev and his crewmate survive the record-breaking stint in space without killing each other. They managed their interpersonal conflicts despite the monumental pressure they were under. An oath that Lebedev made to himself on the day of the space launch may have had something to do with the fact that they survived as friends:

1. "In any difficult situation that might occur on board, I must follow my head, not my heart.

2. I won't speak or act out hastily.

3. If Tolia is in the wrong, I will find it in myself to hold out my hand to him; if I am in the wrong, I will be strong enough to admit it.

4. I will remember that my crewmate also deserves respect because of his hard work. He has good family, friends, and people who believe in him.

5. In any circumstances I will keep my self-control; I will not speak or act harshly.

6. The success of the mission depends on us, and only by the work we both do will they judge me as a cosmonaut and as a man.

7. I believe that I am a strong-willed, intelligent person and can properly complete this mission—I've come a long way to get here."[5]

Lebedev figured out how to minimize conflict in a confined space. He was discerning about when to be careful with his crewmate's feelings, and when to be honest if it was mission critical. But maybe he was being a little too conflict-avoidant for his own mental well-being. Practically every diary entry throughout the 211 days complained about a lousy night's sleep, although that may have had something to do with the fact that they slept like bats in sleeping bags hanging from the space vessel's walls.

Dr. Jay C. Buckey, a physician and former astronaut himself, referenced Lebedev's memoir in a conversation we had about how to manage conflict in isolated conditions, when it's paramount that you maintain the relationships you have with your fellow space travelers. Jay, who traveled aboard a Space Shuttle in 1998 as part of the Neurolab Mission, studied microgravity on the nervous system. Dr. Buckey, who circled the Earth 256 times in 16 days, didn't necessarily experience the same level of tension as the cosmonauts. In the space world, that was more like a weekend getaway!

"But I could see how it could get to that level up there," he recently shared.

That's partly why he's made it his life's mission to help those who live in isolation or confinement manage stress and depression. Through his work at the Space Medicine Innovations Lab at the Geisel School of Medicine, Dartmouth College, Dr. Bucky recreates situations to test practical ways of deescalating tension.

As Dr. Buckey tells it, avoiding conflict is rarely a good strategy. It can cause small issues to escalate. People can attach ill intentions and meaning to remarks and actions that were never intended, but failing to engage or discuss allows the misunderstanding to fester, turning what began as a minor irritation into something that threatens to disrupt or destroy all that you and your crewmates have worked toward.

"In the Russian space program, reports are that three missions had to be terminated due to interpersonal conflict," Dr. Buckey says. "That's significant."

So, in three cases that we know of, the astronauts had to come back down to Earth early, likely at a cost of millions, because the stress levels from unresolved tensions permeated every task in a situation where even the smallest error can be a matter of life and death. Yet these monumental bust-ups can be averted through careful conflict management, "not elimination," Dr. Buckey explains. "Because those issues that were there yesterday will still be there today."

I will share more of the techniques for conflict engagement and resolution recommended by Dr. Buckey's space lab later in this book. But, for now, you need to accept the premise that butting heads is in fact a healthy and authentic way to clear the air, heal relationships, drive creativity, and get results, however noisy and messy it may appear in the process. Don't avoid it. If anything, lean into it. Make it serve a larger purpose. Leverage it to your advantage, because if you can learn to engage in constructive conflict in a confined space, you can handle conflict anytime, anywhere, whether you're stuck on an oil drill in Arctic Alaska or home in quarantine with your domestic partner. Confronting something before it goes nuclear is a skill set worth having for those relationships worth keeping.

Conflict also enforces standards. If an employee or person is acting or performing below the level you expect of your team, you must either accept the lower bar, making peace with reduced expectations, or engage in conflict or discipline to enforce it. I vote for the latter because herein lies a teachable moment, an opportunity to do better. When employees or people around you understand that you will engage in conflict rather than accept reduced performance, people perform. In essence, in those cases, conflict spurs growth and advancement.

Stoke the Creative Fires

Yet, in their squeamishness about conflict, many turn a blind eye to its benefits, like the parents who believe that there should be no scorekeeping at their kids' soccer games. We're in the midst of a great social experiment, the consequences of which we may live to regret. Children who grow up in a world without conflict, who never encounter disagreement or failure, enter their adolescence and adult years woefully unprepared to deal with day-to-day life. Kids who play for teams that don't keep score never have the incentive to try harder. Children who are rewarded for simply being present never learn the rewards of taking a risk. Conflict is a part of life. Better we learn to embrace it than pretend it does not exist.

Innovation and creativity can also grow from conflict when people engage in it wisely. Consider some of the greatest rock and pop bands of all time, whose members often had to hash out creative differences, making iconic music in the process: the Beatles, Queen, the Rolling Stones, Guns N' Roses, Fleetwood Mac . . . Even the Beach Boys were known to have battled over which direction their music should take. Keith Richards and Mick Jagger have long had a combustible relationship, but somehow their "frenemyship" has kept the Rolling Stones' artistic and performance fires burning over these many decades.

It's not always recommended, because many a great act has broken up for good over unresolved conflict, but when these artists engage with one another the right way, leaning into the tension that often rises during passionate collaboration, the result can be true greatness. Each bandmate challenged the other to do better, to play a more powerful chord or construct a more elegant or moving bridge into the next verse of the song.

"Every creative group—the Beatles, Monty Python [. . .] had a lot of internal conflict," Peter Coleman, co-executive director of the Advanced Consortium on Cooperation, Conflict and Complexity at Columbia University told *CBS Sunday Morning* in an interview. "And what they did with that conflict was oftentimes find a better solution. So conflicts can result in fantastic innovation."

Team Tension Solves Problems

In the same way, business teams work better with some well-managed conflict. Collaboration needs differences of opinion in the room; otherwise, what's the point? Some of the greatest ideas come out of heated debate, each participant arguing passionately for their point of view, yet willingly taking in the thoughts of others. That's how creative solutions are born, a fact Mary Barra, the CEO of General Motors, knows all too well, as she and her team have problem-solved successfully through some of the automotive giant's greatest challenges. (Remember the faulty, and deadly, ignition switches?)

"When we have to make tough decisions, giving direction and setting the strategies for the products of General Motors, there should be constructive tension. We should have vigorous debates," she told the *Los Angeles Times* in an interview when she took the helm, adding, "I want that tension in a constructive way to make sure we evaluate things from every angle."[6]

What Barra is describing is constructive conflict in a nutshell. Business leaders are often afraid of the term, but it's an essential ingredient in running a corporation, and its absence can explain many collaborative failures.

"Clashes between parties are the crucibles in which creative solutions are developed and wise trade-offs among competing objectives are made," say Jeff Weiss and Jonathan Hughes in a *Harvard Business Review* article titled "Want Collaboration?: Accept—and Actively Manage—Conflict."[7]

But executives tend to focus on the symptoms, like different departments not working together closely enough, rather than the root cause of failures in the collaborative process—a lack of healthy conflict.

"The fact is, you can't improve collaboration until you've addressed the issue of conflict," the article goes on to say. Conflict is as inevitable as it is important to an organization, "So instead of trying simply to reduce disagreements, senior executives need to embrace conflict and [. . .] institutionalize mechanisms for embracing it."

There is a large and growing body of research on the benefits of conflict, which is becoming a significant new field in academia. Harvard Business School management guru John Kotter says flatly, "To make positive, lasting change, you need to energize people [. . .] And you need conflict to accomplish that."[8]

Whether you're running a company or just running your life, managing relationships with your family members, colleagues, and friends, the same goes. *Don't run from conflict.* Use it as a lever to bring underlying issues to the surface and bring about positive change. Release the pressure valve and point all that energy into a more productive direction.

The Best Medicine

That should be the end goal of all constructive conflict: to make things better. This is as true for a Fortune 100 company as it is for the human body. In fact, avoiding conflict can be bad for your physical health. Conversely, conflict avoidance can cause untold damage to your well-being. Hear me out.

Many assume that to avoid an argument and "keep the peace" reduces stress. Maybe there is a semblance of calm in the short term, but eventually the opposite is true. Swallowing your words over and over again, silencing and suppressing yourself as you tiptoe around topics to avoid igniting an argument can actually become corrosive. It can lead to repressed anger and frustration as your inner turmoil goes unexpressed. You're more likely to relitigate issues, hashing them out in your mind rather than moving forward in a positive way if you don't permit yourself the opportunity to air out your grievances, objections, or concerns. Not only can holding back stifle the kind of communication necessary to maintain healthy relationships, ultimately it can lead to depression, self-esteem issues, and maybe even cognition problems from countless sleepless nights.

But don't take *my* word for it. I have the privilege of knowing a lot of leading scientists and doctors. The more I thought about the case for conflict, the more I wondered if there could be circumstances under which it is physically healthy to step onto the mat, figuratively speaking. Is allowing yourself an old-fashioned dustup actually good for you mentally, physically, and physiologically? So I asked Dr. Marwan Sabbagh, director of the Lou Ruvo Center for Brain Health at the Cleveland Clinic and one of the world's leading neurologists, what he thought about my theory.

"Submissive individuals who constantly put their ideals aside, pacifying, deflecting, and mollifying to avoid conflict, aren't resolving anything; they're simply internalizing it," he told me.

"So what does that do to your brain?" I asked.

"Chemically, where there is unresolved conflict, over time it could affect the brain's neurotransmitters. It impacts not just the fight-or-flight adrenal steroids, but dopamine and serotonin."

In other words, the unease caused by the conflict you bury deep within your being can become constant. By not standing up for yourself, that constant release of cortisol—the stress hormone—can put you in a state of chronic anxiety while inhibiting the release of those feel-good chemicals, sapping the pleasure out of life.

On the flip side: "Resolving personal conflict has major downstream benefits in terms of mood, sleep, and cognition," Dr. Sabbagh told me.

Put another way, meaningful, constructive conflict that can lead to some kind of resolution is the best medicine for your neurological, physical, and emotional health. If interpersonal and internal conflict is the underlying cause of most stress, which it is, then dealing with that conflict will naturally restore a sense of control over the situation and, ultimately, your well-being. Just think back on those times you've "cleared the air" with a friend or loved one, and the relief you felt when you finally released those feelings you've been bottling up. Or recall the adrenaline rush you experienced after a lively debate with a worthy opponent. All those positive emotions wash through your nervous system, restoring your sense of calm.

"There is certainly merit in the theory that managing conflict head-on is healthy," agreed Dr. Justin Miller, a clinical neuropsychologist at the Cleveland Clinic. "If a patient's way of coping is to acquiesce and avoid the conflict, it may help mitigate the near-term discomfort and anxiety that conflict can create. But this avoidance behavior can become self-reinforcing, which creates its own challenges. So talking through the problem and engaging in conflict for the purpose of conflict resolution can be considered a form of proactive anxiety management."

When I put this theory to my friend Dr. Phil McGraw in my podcast, he tended to agree that there is a physiological difference between those who are willing to go to the mat, and those who never fight back.

"Unresolved conflict over time dulls the endorphins or receptors of the brain, which can have a deleterious effect on the rest of the body. Not sticking up for yourself can in fact be unhealthy."

So constructive conflict could even be viewed as a kind of therapy!

Mind over Weight

There's so much more to explore in the physical and mental health link to conflict that it could be another book. Dr. Ian Smith, a TV doc and host of the show *Celebrity Fit Club* who specializes in weight-loss challenges, engages in conflict with countless patients, whose eating disorders are often the result of years of unresolved conflict—unfought battles with family members, society, and themselves . . .

"If you don't address something through meaningful conflict, it can lead to weight loss or gain," Dr. Smith explained. "It results in people medicating themselves and soothing tension through food."

So if you don't speak up at the office when you should, and allow an unacceptable situation to persist, you go home feeling frustrated and reach for the potato chips.

"Most people do this without ever connecting the two behaviors," explained Dr. Smith, whose book, *Mind over Weight*,[9] delves into the vicious cycle of unhealthy weight and unmanaged conflict. "It goes all the way back to childhood for many of my patients, who felt humiliated by their own family members and never felt worthy of sticking up for themselves. They won't allow themselves to engage in any kind of conflict, even if that means being insulted or disrespected."

That's why, as I do on *Bar Rescue*, the good doctor takes a tough love approach when appropriate. He confronts his patients, looking for an opening, "so I can get to the foundation of why they feel the way they feel." It's a long process of digging through old scar tissue to find the source of their low confidence. Sometimes it involves "taking that person down to building them back up again."

Part of Dr. Smith's method involves initiating conflict with patients, forcing them to wrap their heads around the fact that their future may be diabetes, kidney failure, heart problems, and a whole host of other medical issues that will diminish their well-being and shorten their life spans. He makes them see uncomfortable truths they would rather not face, so they can start to unpack the emotional baggage that's causing them to eat their feelings and slowly kill themselves.

"As a physician, I am well aware of the situation they will face if they do not change, so engaging in constructive conflict with my patients, and encouraging my patients to confront themselves and others over the underlying issues, is a big part of my practice."

Purpose-Driven Conflict

So the stakes of conflict, and the failure to engage, can be life-and-death. But the good news is that we, as individuals, can empower ourselves to use these situations to improve not just our own lives, but the world around us.

There are plenty of tools that will enable you to use conflict fairly, positively, and winningly. Healthy engagement is never reactive. It comes from a thoughtful strategy that is executed with intention. There is power in doing conflict right, and I am about to give you a set of tools that will enable you to harness that power with confidence. Again, conflict is not to be avoided, but embraced, harnessed, and put to good purpose.

Successful conflict management is accessible to all of us. These next pages will detail the approaches, techniques, and tricks necessary for engagement in respectful, effective conflict. Once you do begin to practice the art and science of conflict, you will quickly discover its benefits. Engaging in and acknowledging conflict can be a way of clearing the air, of getting to the bottom of issues that, once resolved, can strengthen friendships, lessen political machinations at work, and help form alliances between nations that reduce or eliminate escalating tensions. I call this kind of healthy confrontation "conflict with a purpose" or "deliberate conflict."

What does that look like? The process is never pretty. Ignoring the rules of "political correctness" on my shows, I get in the faces of those I am trying to pull back from the brink of financial ruin, because I care. My voice rises, sometimes to a screeching pitch. This is tough love on steroids. But, as tense as it gets, I am there to save livelihoods, and lives.

Not that I always advise an in-your-face strategy for resolving conflict. In fact, my patented yelling and name-calling is effective in limited situations but is virtually *never* the first-choice solution to settling a dispute. All conflict begins with discussion. Conflict flows from discussion into a point of disagreement, then into conflict. Discussions can end the conflict or escalate it, often without warning or announcement. It is at that juncture, that personally or professionally defining moment, when we each make the choice to succumb to the flow of the discussion or to "step out" of the flow and engage the escalation. With a foundation of respect, a clear objective justifying engagement, and a belief that the conflict can be meaningful, *stepping out becomes stepping up.*

Healthy debate is essential to our democracy. The United States Constitution was the product of intense debate among our founding fathers—some of the greatest minds in human history. But the result was a document that spells out the eternal principles of dignity, freedom, and fairness our nation has lived by for centuries. Many of our most significant scientific, cultural, and social achievements have been the result of an intense dialectic where viewpoints and facts get hashed out with honesty and passion. But a lack of conflict stops everything.

Conversely, approaching conflict and meaningful discussion with confidence creates positive momentum. It can change minds, engage others, and create the energy necessary to move forward, whether individually or on the world stage. Yes, it can get messy. But the alternative could be far worse.

A World without Conflict

So where would we be today without conflict? Well, the fear of going against some of the most popular narratives of the day is creating some disturbingly one-sided conversations. Many otherwise intelligent and well-meaning leaders and media pundits seem to have forgotten that some of our greatest legislative accomplishments are the result of the fierce conflict on the floor of Congress, in the polls, and in ground movements of political and social campaigns.

Consider what happens in *Star Trek*'s famed episode, "The City on the Edge of Forever." Captain Kirk, Spock, and Dr. McCoy travel back in time to save the universe. How? By making sure that World War II happens. The story takes place in 1930s New York, where a charismatic social worker, played by Joan Collins, passionately believes in peace and nonviolence. She somehow convinces the US to stay out of the war brewing in Europe. As a result, history is changed, the Nazis win, and the world we live in today does not exist. In order to save the world, Kirk and his crew must go back in time to stop the social worker's crusade for peace to ensure that the United States becomes embroiled in a conflict that rages for years.

It's hardly surprising that this is one of the most beloved *Star Trek* episodes of all time, even among non-Trekkies like me. Under the guise of science fiction and hokey 1960s TV entertainment, it poses the complex question: Is conflict to be avoided at all costs, no matter how high the price?

The fate of the universe does not have to be at stake for us to know that the answer to that question is a resounding *no*. Yet many of us cut and run rather than face disagreements head-on, or we give in to the other side and compromise our beliefs and values. This is not a strategy for happiness in life or success in business.

Again, the latest research is coming to the same conclusion, comparing unacknowledged conflict to hypertension: "left untreated, such strife can, like high blood pressure that remains ignored, cause lasting damage to organizational health and performance."[10]

Social scientists and organizational psychologists are just now learning how trust between the parties in conflict erodes when their disagreements are not brought out into the open for resolution; how failure to confront underperforming employees is a pathway to business failure; and, most important, how quashing conflict for the sake of false harmony in the workplace stifles the spirit of innovation and entrepreneurship.

We are seeing this unhealthy passive aggression play out in countless scenarios. Like at one college campus on Halloween night when a group of students thought it would be fun to dress up and stroll the campus in costume. One of the young men, who stood tall at six five, went as Snow White, and recruited a few of his shorter friends to go with him as Sneezy, Grumpy, and Doc. They were quite a sight. But it wasn't so funny the next morning when they were summoned to the dean's office. It seems they'd offended a classmate who promptly reported them to the dean. No one was sure exactly what had caused the hurt feelings. The classmate never said a word directly to the "offending" students—but instead went running to the authorities.

College kids are known for breaking the rules, for testing the limits of just how far their peers and their social and academic milieu will let them stray from the norm. We've all done it, and we've all learned a lesson or two along the way. As adults, we generally know which buttons to push to stir up disagreement, and which ones to leave alone because the ensuing chaos is just not worth the rigmarole. In other words—we provoke conflict, and we learn from its aftermath. In this case, though, it was difficult for the students in question to figure out exactly which rules they'd broken.

So imagine a world in which engaging in conflict is not permitted, because the minute you push that button, the law swoops in and clamps down on you and your itchy button finger. In fact, we may already be living in that world. A poll taken by College Pulse found that 51 percent of college students think fellow students should be punished for wearing inappropriate costumes. Of course, no student *should* wear a truly offensive costume. Blackface, for example, clearly has a racist history and its only purpose would be to cause offense and taunt others with its painful past. But there is a big difference between encouraging students to be respectful of others in their costume choice and *punishing* people for wearing something that is unintentionally triggering. One response is reasonable, and the other is not.

Do not pass go. Do not collect $200. Go directly to jail. This dystopia is the future of a world in which conflict is forbidden. Where your right to disagree with somebody else's poor judgment is forestalled by automatic censure. Do we really want to live in a society in which we are not free to disagree? One in which we do not even speak to people whose opinions differ from ours, but instead go running to an authority figure to make it (whatever "it" is) better? Or would we rather live in a world in which we build norms by working through a series of disagreements to the mutual satisfaction of ourselves and those with whom we disagree?

You already know the answer. If you think the costs of conflict are too high, prepare to be bankrupted in business and in life by the price of avoiding it. Expect your worldview to get steamrolled.

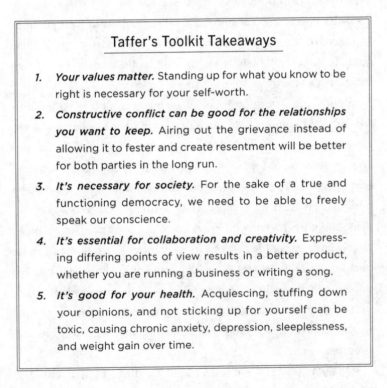

Taffer's Toolkit Takeaways

1. *Your values matter.* Standing up for what you know to be right is necessary for your self-worth.

2. *Constructive conflict can be good for the relationships you want to keep.* Airing out the grievance instead of allowing it to fester and create resentment will be better for both parties in the long run.

3. *It's necessary for society.* For the sake of a true and functioning democracy, we need to be able to freely speak our conscience.

4. *It's essential for collaboration and creativity.* Expressing differing points of view results in a better product, whether you are running a business or writing a song.

5. *It's good for your health.* Acquiescing, stuffing down your opinions, and not sticking up for yourself can be toxic, causing chronic anxiety, depression, sleeplessness, and weight gain over time.

2

THE FIGHT IN MY HEAD

*Embrace internal conflict. Fire-test your position
with new information and opposing views.*

Each time Rosemary got off the phone with her elderly father, she felt a tinge of sadness. He lived on the other side of the country and most years she would fly to visit him at least a couple of times. But, because of the risks involved from the global pandemic, the two couldn't meet face-to-face, so she checked in with him by phone three to four times a week. Meanwhile, Dad tuned in to one of the twenty-four-hour cable channels for all his information about the outside world. There, inside his little COVID bubble, he was inadvertently indoctrinating himself, soaking up a particular partisan viewpoint on everything from lockdowns to vaccines to Meghan Markle and Prince Harry like an addicted sponge.

Of course, this was not Rosemary's perspective on what was going on in the world. A small-business owner who had no choice but to travel and interact with the rest of society, she found her opinions moving further and further away from her father's. She felt frustrated by the lockdowns and questioned the way specific restrictions were being applied, for example. She felt it was healthy in a democratic society to debate the issues and push back on bureaucratic overreach when safe and responsible to do so. Rosemary had all along assumed that this attitude was bipartisan. But it got to the point where she would innocently mention a topic, not even realizing it was political, and provoke outrage in the housebound octogenarian. Without ever intending to upset her father, she often found herself on the defensive, trying to justify her position.

To avoid the next conflict, Rosemary started censoring herself, keeping subjects of conversation as neutral and superficial as possible, like the weather or what her dad planned to eat for dinner. Soon she felt she could no longer share her true feelings with her beloved parent. Tiptoeing through the minefield made her feel as if she were losing that connection with the gentle, caring, and intelligent man who had raised her. They soon ran out of neutral topics to discuss, and three phone calls a week whittled down to one.

It's a problem so many families faced during these fraught and divisive times. Fathers and daughters, mothers and sons, brothers and sisters, kith and kin were either walking on eggshells with each other to avoid sparking an argument or getting into it with a no-holds-barred passion that turned into anger, then resentment, then estrangement. For the first time in living memory, loved ones were canceling each other out of their lives for the way they voted or the opinions they held.

Channel Surfing

But Rosemary was determined not to let this happen. She decided to break the stalemate with her dad and find some common ground. Although she disagreed with her pop and the pundits who influenced him, she challenged herself to listen. For three days before her next call, she made herself watch his favorite news channels, and read all the newspapers and media websites she could find that leaned his way. She found some of the content extremely annoying at first, but she persisted, training herself to not react so emotionally to what she was hearing. She sat still with it, comparing their perspectives with her own as dispassionately as she could.

The more she listened, the more she put her own ideas to the test. While Rosemary didn't necessarily agree with the pundits on the other networks, she could see how, if that was all her father was exposed to, he would hold certain views. She recognized that the spin and emphasis of the news anchors and commentators on her preferred channels and social media feeds were slanting certain stories and factoids. She also realized that much of the commentary was designed to divide us, as if there were no room for any but two extreme and opposite opinions.

After a few weeks, Rosemary began viewing things through a whole new lens. She took a more neutral position on some topics and became more open to hearing another perspective—her father's. She even adjusted her opinions on a few issues, like stimulus spending and immigration reform.

During their next conversation, Rosemary decided to venture into those sensitive topics with her dad. But, instead of declaring her opinions from the outset of the conversation, she asked him how he felt. Instead of disagreeing or giving in to a knee-jerk response, she paused for a moment to deeply consider what he was saying. Then she followed up, quoting one of his favorite anchors. It gave her dad a sense of validation, and the conversation continued, with Rosemary expressing points of agreement but also subtly relating her own experiences and inserting her more moderate opinions.

Warming to the subject and softened by his daughter's openness, Dad conceded a few small points, ventured to ask her about her own views, and the two finally managed to find some common ground. It made their conversations more engaging, as they not only shared opinions on the news of the day, but jokes and fond family memories. Father and daughter found themselves looking forward to their two-, three-, or four-times weekly phone calls.

Flex the Contradiction Muscle

Rosemary was practicing a form of internal conflict that I consider essential groundwork for healthy engagement. She was intentionally exposing herself to ideas that didn't necessarily sit comfortably with her in an effort to become more expansive in her thinking.

This is something I urge all of you to do before I take you on this journey of constructive conflict. Just as fighters need to build muscle and get to fighting weight before they even think about stepping into the ring, running, jumping rope, doing squats, or sparring with the punching bag, you need to build up your own internal engagement muscles. You need to do the floor work and resistance workouts so you can be strong, flexible, and quick on your feet. Some quick exercises to get you fighting fit for the arena of ideas include:

- Taking your TV remote and doing as Rosemary did: flick over to the other stations. If you're a CNN or MSNBC watcher, dare to switch to Fox News for a few minutes, or as long as you can stomach. Start with someone moderate like Chris Wallace or Harris Faulkner and build up to Tucker Carlson (i.e., maybe don't start with the primetime anchors). Likewise, on CNN, begin with Wolf Blitzer or NBC's Chuck Todd before venturing into Joy Reid or Rachel Maddow territory. Baby steps!

- Similarly, adding some variety to your newspaper- and magazine-reading diet.

- Chatting with friends with whom you agree to disagree. But don't try to win the argument. Just listen and probe, asking open-ended questions and sitting with the answers as you try to understand your friends better.

- And watching their social media feeds. You'll be amazed at the difference in information they are getting. We are all being fed a constant stream of opinion-affirming and often questionable claims, whichever end of the political spectrum we stand on (more on that later).

Opinion Rut

Right now, thanks to social media, our internal development has become stunted. We are living in an age where we're getting locked in our own opinions. Few of us are exposed to a media that brings a balance of views and information. Today's 24/7 news and social media are designed to do little more than bolster the beliefs we already hold dear, bombarding us with opinions and exposing us to part-truths and outright distortion.

We've grown soft because we're not challenging ourselves to push past this constant stream, which leaves us trapped in a mindset and closed off to anyone or anything that might threaten our cherished worldview, and the result is a stagnation of ideas. How can we possibly grow when we aren't capable of an internal dialogue? How can we digest new information for a more nuanced perspective, or evolve in our thinking, when we won't allow the slightest contradictions into our thought space? And how can we effectively engage and communicate with others when our minds are not only made up, they've atrophied?

The ability to have an internal conflict, and possibly even change our minds on a particular subject, is a hugely underrated skill. Being able to accept new data that changes our positions is strength, not weakness, and it enhances our mental agility as we countenance and debate the onslaught of opinions, information, and misinformation that are out there. It enables us to defend our core beliefs more effectively while also listening to one another with greater compassion. So we owe it to ourselves and those we care about to strengthen our ability to receive and wrestle with ideas we don't like.

Not that it's always a comfortable process. The psychological term for holding thoughts or engaging in behavior that is inconsistent with our beliefs is "cognitive dissonance." The phrase is often equated with that unpleasant feeling we get when we know we're supposed to be watching our cholesterol, for example, but we just finished gorging ourselves on a juicy cheeseburger with fries. It's that moment when you recognize that you are holding conflicting beliefs, or your behavior contradicts those beliefs. As a result, we take steps to try to eliminate the dissonance, like self-justification, denial, dismissal. . . . So we tell ourselves we'll eat clean and go for a jog the next morning to resolve the dissonance.

Garbage In; Garbage Out

Cognitive dissonance can also happen when a set of facts is introduced that disrupts the narrative we've chosen for ourselves. Of course, in the age of social media, it's become much easier to make those uncomfortable feelings of internal conflict go away. We can always decide to listen to the chorus on our Facebook and Twitter feeds to reinforce our preexisting set of beliefs and drown out the inconvenient data. As the Netflix documentary *The Social Dilemma* made clear, sophisticated algorithms based on past clicks, searches, and views ensure we are given content that not only agrees with our habitual stances on certain issues, but leads us down a path where even the most outlandish conspiracy theories can seem plausible. We can choose our own set of facts and dismiss the contradicting source of the information as biased and choose to ignore or avoid further information that challenges existing beliefs. This filtered data doesn't allow us to view the other side as objectively as we should, causing us to dig in even more.

But another response to cognitive dissonance can be the desire to reconcile the disagreeable information. It can inspire us to take the new information on board and adjust our opinions or behavior. This healthier response of leaning into the data that makes us uncomfortable leads to internal growth, better decision-making, and greater self-awareness, explains psychiatrist Grant H. Brenner MD, FAPA, co-founder of Neighborhood Psychiatry in New York City. It's an opportunity to become more in tune with our core values and more aligned with them.

"Developing a sense of inner conflict is a good thing to notice," he says, "because . . . if competing values, beliefs, attitudes, etc. are not resolved or integrated, it greatly inhibits the ability of groups to have constructive dialogue, making it difficult, if not impossible, to arrive at a satisfactory compromise."[1]

So internal conflict, and that icky feeling of cognitive dissonance that arises from it, is an opportunity for growth. It makes us more elastic in our thinking, and objective in our decision-making. It forces us to face facts we don't like and address or resolve them in some way. I like to think of it as that bit of grit that floats into an oyster's shell. Over time, the oyster coats that irritating speck until it becomes an iridescent pearl. That inner conflict can eventually build into a pearl of wisdom.

The early-nineteenth-century American theologian William Ellery Channing put it another way: "Difficulties are meant to rouse, not discourage. The human spirit is to grow strong by conflict."

Darn right it can. But first you have to open up your shell and let it in.

Embrace the Contrarian

On the flip side, if you never allow yourself the opportunity to understand the opposing view, how can you ever expect to fully come to grips with an issue that's important to you? How do we make the best decisions for ourselves? All views change as we go through experiences and mature. Or at least they should. If we never allow for the possibility that we might be wrong about a subject, how do we maintain an intelligent position on something when we're out in society? And how do we argue a point with confidence if we haven't first allowed ourselves to put it through the fire test within our own consciousness? Once we have properly defined our position on issues, we should welcome engagement with others, not fear it. But it starts within. We can only build up our confidence and powers of external conflict when we've been able to have it out with ourselves.

Recognize that most subjects worth your mental bandwidth tend to be multifaceted, not binary. Take the hot-button issue of immigration, for example. Most people can agree they want people to come to the United States to live a better life. Americans recognize that we are a melting pot, and that cultural diversity makes us better in many ways. But there is vehement disagreement over the various pathways to citizenship and how open we want our borders to be. How we arrive at a solution is fraught with intense internal debate.

As human beings, we are bound to change our opinions on many things over a lifetime. That's called growth. Think about the things you would have said or done when you were eighteen and compare that to your perspective now that you are a responsible young professional in your thirties, or a parent of an eighteen-year-old in your fifties, and so on. Think about some of the decisions you might have made then, like quitting school to go backpacking through Southeast Asia, for example. As a middle-aged mother or father with two kids to put through school, that seems risky now, doesn't it? While it may seem all right for some to smoke pot, trek through land-mine-ridden hillsides, and jump into the Mekong River in Laos, your life circumstances have changed. What could once be described as an adventure is now reckless and irresponsible.

I've changed my own political position over the years. As a young man, I was all for social programs. Taxing and spending made sense to me. But, as a businessman, my position on government spending became more nuanced. Direct experience as an employer and hefty taxpayer made me much more fiscally conservative. I came to believe that a slightly smaller government, with more of our hard-earned dollars in our pockets, was better for us as an economy and as a nation. I could see the direct benefits of having more cash to reinvest in my businesses and in my employees, who could in turn improve the lives of their own families and communities. To be clear, I am still as socially liberal as they come, and proactively supportive of LGBTQ, civil, and women's rights. So you would be hard-pressed to put me in any kind of box. I don't belong on either side of the partisan divide, and, if you really think about it, you probably don't sit comfortably alongside any extreme political ideology either.

Again, opinions can and must change. It's how we evolve as individuals. But if we are only exposing ourselves to slanted data or segmented information, how can we engage in internal conflict? How can we make informed decisions or become compassionate people who recognize those on the other side as fellow humans who may, on occasion, make a good point? We are remiss when we do not receive the opposing view or attempt to come to grips with information we don't like.

In my own life and career there have been countless occasions when I've had to consider a point of view when I believed I was already well informed on a subject. A few years ago, while on the set of *Bar Rescue*, someone said something that was perceived as a slant against LGBTQ individuals, even though that was not how the remark was intended. To be clear, I didn't say it. But to make things right, my crew and I were required to sit through a four-hour education session by GLAAD.

At first, I was offended. "How dare they think I need this!" I said to myself. I don't oppose anyone's lifestyle and considered myself to be as nondiscriminatory as anyone. But then I made a decision to go into it with a positive attitude and an open mind. I showed up and fully listened. To my surprise, that four-hour discussion was powerful. It taught me that there was much more I could do in terms of creating a sensitive workplace. It helped me realize that none of us is perfect and we all do things unconsciously that could hurt someone, even when we don't intend to cause offense. Allowing myself to hear ideas from a new perspective, even when I believed I already knew it all, expanded my thinking and made me realize that the issue was more complex and multifaceted than I had thought. It was a gift.

Probe versus Pushback

There are many other ways I introduce new and opposing ideas into my thinking, helping me to build up my internal conflict muscles. Professionally and personally, I surround myself with people who have diverse opinions. I lived for years in Hollywood, so I have several close friends in the film and entertainment industry who are far more left of center than I happen to be. They know that I tend to be center of center on some issues, and slightly right of center on others, and it makes for lively dinner conversations. Our discussions might get loud, but they aren't combative. We create a safe space for ourselves to talk openly and agree to disagree and laugh at ourselves while doing so.

But, for me, there's a serious objective to these fun debates. I really want to know why people I love and respect happen to have come to opposite conclusions on certain issues. Because these individuals are important to me, I can't just outright dismiss their opinions. Long after they've left the dinner party, I make a point of going over our exchange and examining what they had to say from all angles. Not only does it sharpen me for our next friendly competition, the thought process that ensues—or the cognitive dissonance that I allow to happen for myself—enables me to come up with more nuanced opinions.

Similarly, I enjoy the fact that my company's vice president and chief of staff, Sean Walker, is an extremely bright millennial who leans left. Sean often disagrees with me, and I always want to know why. I don't push back or get offended. Having him in my orbit is my opportunity to get an honest perspective from someone who represents a hugely important demographic to our business. We may never fully agree on certain subjects, yet hearing what he has to say about a wide range of issues helps me to better understand the other side's point of view. Again, my absolute trust in Sean's intentions and intelligence makes me open my ears. Receiving his opinions and holding them in my mind without prejudgment enables me to build some flexibility and compassion into my thinking on some of the most inflammatory of the day's news headlines.

We all need these kinds of mental circuit breakers to keep us from heading toward extremes. We all need to become more proactive in building our internal conflict skills. The middle ground is getting squeezed harder than ever, putting us into dangerous territory. Extremists can be prevented from taking control only when the middle talks, but the middle is being silenced into nonexistence.

When I was growing up, I watched anchors like Walter Cronkite and Edward R. Murrow deliver the news of the day with an impartial gravitas. We all felt we could trust their presentation of the facts because that was all it was—facts. They reported on what was happening dispassionately, without spin, and presented essential information within the full context. But now all we see are bullies in their pulpits who feel entitled to their own facts, but only when those "facts" support their argument of the moment.

We're living in an accuracy and objectivity vacuum, so it's incumbent upon us to step up, gather all the fragments of information we can, and piece them together for ourselves. Throughout that process, internal conflict can help. Whenever we start questioning a closely held belief instead of resting comfortably in a self-satisfied sense of righteousness, we are inching our way back toward that ever more elusive truth, which often lands us somewhere in the middle, flecked with honest, old-fashioned self-doubt. I want you to trust this nonlinear and sometimes messy self-talk. That internal struggle we feel is a sign of progress.

Of course, I am not necessarily saying you *should* change your mind. Rather, I want you to hone your position. Challenge yourself internally so that your stance is bulletproof. Discard whatever is less defensible and focus only on the points that stand up to examination, developing them until they are laser sharp. Bringing discordant ideas into your headspace will help you clear out the distractions and prevent you from going down rabbit holes. That inner debate will ultimately prepare you to win the arguments that matter most. But first you need to take an inventory of your positions on certain subjects, ensuring that your convictions truly are yours.

As I write this, the world is just coming out of a devastating epidemic and more than a year of lockdowns and isolation. If anything, the fact that most people have been living and communicating in front of digital screens 24/7 has hardened their positions on certain subjects even more. Unable to be in the same room with those whose opinions differ and look those people in the eye, we are left without any real human intervention to counter the narratives as the information coming at us becomes increasingly biased. We are sucking up whatever is in these social feed bubbles and staying with the herd on either side of the political and ideological divide.

Believe me, it's intentional. Big Tech can indoctrinate and manipulate us by delivering confirmation bias after confirmation bias to our laptops before we've even had a chance to finish our first cup of morning joe. The more predictable our behavior becomes, the more they can control our decision-making on not just what to click or view, but where to spend and how to vote. It's much more sinister than just being able to sell our data to advertisers. It's a power move that ultimately gives these and other corporations more riches and control. They're rigging the game.

But you have the power to stop this trajectory. Starting from within, you can become the disrupter of the narratives that others want to impose on you. By continually practicing internal debate, you are effectively fighting back. You're also preparing yourself for external conflict when it finally comes to you. By that time, you will have the confidence of your convictions because you'll have put them through the test of fire inside your own mind.

Now bring it on!

Taffer Toolkit Takeaways

1. *Intentionally expose yourself to opposing views,* be they on social media, via channel surfing, or by reading newspapers and magazines that you know to have different ideological stances. Try to stay open, searching for at least one thing you can agree with on the opposite side, or at least understand how someone might come to that conclusion.

2. *Don't react. Receive.* Consciously let the opposing fact or opinion sit with you for a few uncomfortable minutes, or more. Hold the thoughts in your mind and examine them from all possible sides. Sleep on it!

3. *Think of an issue you feel strongly about, then make a list of points for and points against.* Look at the two columns to see which points come closest to agreement, then list those views in between the for and against. There's your middle ground!

4. *Surround yourself with people who you respect but who don't necessarily share all your opinions.* Pick a topic for a friendly debate in a safe space, all the while agreeing to disagree. Listen carefully to arguments and challenge yourself to find common ground. When the discussion is over, think for a while about what they had to say. You don't have to agree, but you can try to understand or at least step back and contemplate. Have these conversations routinely.

5. *If a subject comes up and you find someone disagrees with you, lean into it.* Probe them further, seek new information, and draw out their opinions with follow-up questions. Don't try to argue. Just be curious and open. Again, receive.

3

PICK YOUR BATTLES

Assess when conflict is necessary and constructive, and when to walk away.

The toxic mix of personalities dominating the decision-making on her North Carolina condo board was the last thing Clarissa wanted to deal with. She'd long suspected there was some level of malfeasance going on with the board officers, who'd been running things for more than a decade, but she figured that petty corruption was the way of most of these condo boards, so she resigned herself to the status quo. If that was the price to pay to avoid dealing with these people, so be it.

Then one day she got word that the perks may have gone beyond extra influence over what paint color to use in the lobby or who gets a coveted parking space. One of her neighbors noticed some suspicious price inflation for some major contracting work that needed to be done on the building. She began to wonder if the difference between the price that building owners were paying and the actual cost of the work was going into certain board executives' pockets, ultimately forcing elderly owners with fixed incomes to choose between paying their inflated HOA dues and assessment fees or filling their prescriptions.

Deeply concerned, Clarissa raised the matter in an email to the board. The board executives quickly closed ranks and went on the counterattack, issuing baseless fines against her and generally letting her know who was in charge around there, and the financial punishment for anyone who dared to question it. But there was a board election coming up, a chance to bring in some new blood. Rather than get mad, Clarissa decided to get even.

She went on a fact-finding mission, canvassing door-to-door to get to know her neighbors and learn about their concerns. She got an earful of stories about the bullying tactics of the board executives and quickly discovered that enough of her neighbors were like-minded and willing to step up and form a slate to take over the board.

Catching wind of the insurrection, the board president, we'll call her Bula, decided to write a stream of nasty emails cc'd to the entire building full of lies and ad hominem attacks on Clarissa's character. The invective was so extreme and so out of touch with reality that Clarissa wondered if Bula had some kind of borderline personality disorder. She'd scarcely had any direct dealings with the woman until she made that challenge to her in a group email to the board, which was even and professional in tone. But you would never know it from Bula's vitriolic reaction. The question was, should Clarissa answer these attacks in person at the next board meeting?

She ultimately decided not to engage with Bula. Acknowledging these ridiculous attacks would only give them the credence they did not deserve. Instead, she and her co-candidates decided to run a positive campaign promising greater transparency and a kinder, gentler tone in the building. They won by a landslide. Bula and her corrupt cohorts were enraged, but, like a parent who lets her toddler scream and stamp his feet in the grocery store aisle, Clarissa knew it was only a matter of time before they would tire themselves out.

Step Over the Viper Pit

I share this story with you because it demonstrates that not all conflict is created equal. Deciding who to engage with, and under what circumstances, is the first step in my Taffer Toolkit for Constructive Conflict. It takes energy to do this right, and some folks simply do not deserve your bandwidth. Positive conflict must start with good faith and a belief that you can change the mind or position of your adversary. It's about improving the relationship or the situation through a dialogue, albeit an intense one, and for that it helps to have a level of respect for the person you are going up against.

Bula was not a worthy adversary for Clarissa. Nothing Clarissa could have done or said to this woman directly would have made a difference to the running of the building. Would it have been ego-gratifying to tear Bula a new one face-to-face? Perhaps. But joining Bula in the viper pit would have done little or nothing to further Clarissa's goal of stopping the mismanagement of the condo community. Clarissa stepped up in a way that did not necessitate individual confrontation, not because she was conflict-avoidant, but because it was the smart move. Taking the high road won Clarissa the respect, and votes, of her neighbors. Working collectively and strategically with some of the more engaged unit owners accomplished the change that the vast majority wanted to see.

So before you step into the conflict arena, ask yourself the following questions:

- What's my ultimate goal? At the end of this exchange, what would I like to be accomplished?
- Is the person or group I am at odds with capable of reason? Are they too entrenched in their own positions to budge? Their opinion may be different from my own, but if I get the

opportunity to make my case, is it even possible to get them to come around to my way of thinking?

- Is my opponent the type of person who likes to argue for argument's sake? Is he inclined to shriek and yell over me just to win and have the last word? Does she twist my words and spew ad hominem attacks that have nothing to do with the issue at hand?

- Is the other party so conflict-avoidant that he'll just yes me until I go away or drop the subject, then continue along the same path?

- Does the potential for collateral damage and pain for those outside the ring outweigh the positive potential outcome of the conflict?

- Is this a long-term relationship where I will need to come together and find a level of harmony following the conflict?

- Is there an alternative way to sideline unworthy opponents and achieve my goals without engaging in a heated exchange that is unlikely to get them to change their views?

I am not saying that your first reflex should be to avoid the confrontation. Hell no! This is about making sure your energy is spent wisely and that you are entering the arena for a just cause. Learn to recognize when someone is immovable. Understand their conflict style. Stand up for yourself, but, if someone is a fool, don't engage at their level. If your opponent is passive-aggressive and turns everything into an excuse for victimhood, don't bother. If the person on the other side of the confrontation is dismissive, hurling insults then running away from the conversation just so that he can have the last word, to heck with him! When they are not willing to fight fair, when they're incapable of listening or taking in what you're trying to say, their words, actions, and body language will tell you so. You'll know soon enough that you're not going to be heard.

Shut It Down!

And, if not, do as I have done countless times on my shows. Shut it down! That's what I had to do in one notable episode of *Marriage Rescue*. In this series, I forced conflict to get couples to open up about underlying issues so that they could work together toward resolving them (more on that later). That strategy almost always ended in success. But one couple entered the arena, or at least one-half of that couple, with no intention of fixing anything.

Bill and Lina had been together for more than twenty years, but for the last several years of the relationship, Bill kept saying he no longer loved Lina. Not only did Lina put up with it, she convinced herself that it was just a phase. But as his drumbeat of threats to leave got louder and more frequent, they decided to come on my show. The more time I spent with the two of them, the more I realized that Lina was partly right: Bill didn't really intend to carry out his threat. It was a power play to keep her submissive. She took such great care of him, and put up with so much of his crap, continuing to be his doormat and sex partner despite the lousy way he treated her.

After taking them through a few exercises to help the relationship, Bill wasn't budging from his stance. But Lina was starting to show some strength. At our next meeting, she told Bill it was time to make up his mind.

"Leave if you're going to leave," she finally told him. "Make your mind up."

When Bill continued to evade, I laid it out for Lina:

"He enjoys the power over you and you live for his next demand."

Linda nodded in agreement.

"Your goodness keeps him; otherwise, he'd have left by now."

To Bill, I said, "Any other normal wife with less commitment than Lina will tell you to go screw yourself!"

Then I told Lina, "See how when you speak, he doesn't like it? You enable him, Lina."

My exposing this truth enraged Bill. He started screaming at me and shouting over Lina.

"Stop interrupting and let her talk," I yelled back. "I am fighting for her. Be a man and tell her what you want to do!"

Bill's belligerence continued. By then it was obvious that this was just a game to him, and a chance for a free vacation in Puerto Rico. He wasn't going to change his behavior and, sadly, it looked like Lina was going to continue to put up with his constant stream of put-downs and humiliation. So I walked away with this final parting shot:

"You are a selfish ass! You don't fight for your wife at all!"

Bill was a bully, plain and simple. He wasn't worth my time, or Lina's. To the best of my knowledge, they are still together, following the same unhealthy pattern.

Oxygen Thieves

I'd say 80 percent of the population *are* worthy adversaries, but there's that 20 percent who are always going to suck the oxygen out of the room, making positive conflict impossible. You can feel it when you are around these people. The very thought of having a deep and meaningful discussion with them leaves you feeling drained. They don't fight fair and they have no interest in reaching common ground. They want affirmation or vindication. They are only in it to win it.

So trust your instincts, nod politely, and change the subject. There is nothing to be gained by opening yourself up to these loonies. Constructive, purposeful conflict isn't about getting attention, scoring a point, or gaining ego gratification. It may be for them, but not for you. You're better than that.

How to Know When to Go Toe-to-Toe

If you're on the fence about whether or not to engage . . .

First, write up a simple pros and cons list. What are the upsides and downsides of direct engagement? There's nothing like putting pen to paper for clearing your head and crystallizing your position on an issue, or its level of urgency. Is it going to matter in five minutes, five days, five months, or five years?

Second, if you've known your prospective adversary for some time, if there's some history there, think back on your relationship. Was there ever a point where you were in agreement on an issue? Can you leverage some common ground for fair and constructive combat?

Third, envision yourself in the ring. Imagine how the discussion is going to go, the points you will raise, and their possible rebuttals. Knowing what you know about the circumstances leading to the conflict as well as the mindset and past actions of the individual on the other side, do you feel pumped and ready to go up against that person? If so, knock 'em dead!

Again, factor in the cost benefit of a confrontation. Consider those instances when the conflict is just not worth it, whether it's making the difficult decision to end a friendship with a "toxic" relationship or extricating yourself from situations that have the potential to turn violent. I made that decision in a famous *Bar Rescue,* or, more precisely, a bar *non-rescue.* During the fourth season of the series, I visited O'Face. The owners were indifferent to customers and employees alike; the employees didn't care much for their colleagues or their customers. Everyone's tempers were short.

I soon discovered violence was being committed on the premises and there had been several criminal complaints against the business.

The pivotal moment came when I observed a video of one of the owners hitting an employee in the face. He then offered to pay one staff member an extra $10 an hour to put another through a glass window! My tolerance for an employer laying a hand on an employee, whether it's a slap or a shove, is exactly zero, so I got out of my SUV and marched into the back alley, where the atrocity was taking place.

"Your bar isn't what's wrong—your character is what's wrong!" I yelled at the husband-and-wife duo. "The problem is you guys are okay with this. You're a mess! You don't need a bar professional—you need a counselor!"

It was the first *Bar Rescue* episode I ever walked out on. We shut that one down for good. I didn't need to rescue a bar then read in the paper the next week that someone got hurt. I didn't want that on my conscience. The risk of engaging in conflict with this owner was just too high: it would have meant putting the *Bar Rescue* crew and myself in harm's way. Again, it just wasn't worth it. Conflict revealed the truth, but there was no purpose to further engagement. Someone else could have been harmed—so, no, not worth it.

During Season Five, the owner of Press Box near Wrigley Field in Chicago, "Smilin' Ed" Cressy, was another hopeless case. We were already pretty far into the taping when I decided to walk away. When I got there, this run-of-the-mill sports bar dive was infested with fruit flies. During the off-season, when the area wasn't rife with Cubs fans, the bar lost between $30,000 to $40,000, so we needed to come up with a concept and a menu that would make it more of a destination year-round.

We changed the name from the Dugout to the Press Box to create a retro 1940s vibe, with a nod to the old-timey sports reporters who covered the games. We built a sleek wooden bar with antique typewriter accents and upgraded the menu and cocktail list. We also installed a state-of-the-art point of sales system to track sales and inventory, to make sure they weren't losing out on liquor sales by excessive pours and too many shots behind the bar.

Smilin' Ed fought me every step of the way. He was brash and arrogant, though nothing I couldn't handle. The dealbreaker for me was that he was a drunk. That's the worst thing you can be when you own a bar, because you're likely to drink your own profits, and then some. Liquor took away his self-control and made him belligerent toward his staff.

Every failing bar has a failing owner, but I'm almost always able to help these individuals recognize what they're doing wrong and how they can fix it. When I engage and offer them tough love advice, there is a breakthrough moment. The recognition often comes by the evening of the big reveal, after my team has worked day and night to give the bar a complete makeover. But when a crowd of more than a hundred people gathered in front of the bar, waiting to see the new look of the Press Box exterior and interior, Smilin' Ed showed up drunk out of his mind and smelling like a distillery.

As he lurched toward me for a sweaty hug, I stepped back and put my hand up.

"You're drunk, aren't you," I told him.

"No, not at all," he lied.

"I can smell it from here!"

(He was standing several feet away from me at that point.)

"My issue is, I can't endorse you; you will suck the life out of everything."

He mumbled something about wanting to run thirty-six bars from Costa Rica.

"There's your bar," I told him, quietly and calmly. "Run it, take the signs down, change the name. . . . Do whatever you want. I'm leaving."

Then I turned to his bar staff, who'd been putting up with years of his nonsense.

"Tell them what you want to do, guys."

"I quit!" said one of the bartenders, then one by one they all walked away, and so did I.

So violence is a dealbreaker. Drunken stupidity is another. And I'll shut it down for good when faced with pure negativity, when a bar owner absolutely refuses to accept my advice despite the fact that I am there because they asked for my help in the first place.

Drunk on Punk

In our fourth season, I tried to rescue the Black Light District lounge in Long Beach, California. It was a live band venue once popular with the punk rock scene, but it was poorly managed, dated, and bleeding cash. The owner, David Franich, had taken investor money, was $160,000 in debt and two months from closing, yet he was mind-blowingly arrogant. When I suggested we freshen things up and offer a more sophisticated cocktail menu, he balked and said, "I know you think you know where you're at, but those fruit loop drinks aren't going to fly over here," reacting to our top mixologists' recipes like some homophobic knucklehead.

"Why are you so negative?" I asked him. "You want me to do what *you* want to do!"

"You can't come here and talk to me like some scumbag," he replied.

"You're the idiot," I informed him. "It's on you. Your ego will destroy anything."

"Go back to the airport and fly the fuck out of here!" he said, looking as if he were getting ready to throw something at me.

I was more than happy to do just that. My biggest pet peeve is having my years of experience and success insulted and dismissed, especially when an owner is failing doing it his way and won't even help himself by listening with respect.

"Good luck on your corner," I said, with one parting shot. "Punks have an edge, but they're not assholes!"

The man was not worthy of my energy. There needs to be something inside the person I go into battle with that I can respect—a shred of decency, humility, a desire for growth . . . something. So I didn't give the episode a second thought until someone informed me that the lounge closed less than a year later, in July 2018. Interestingly, months after I'd turned my back, Franich was still fighting me on social media, answering every critical comment directed at him by *Bar Rescue* fans. Posting on Facebook, he had to have the last word on the day he closed, long past the point when anybody cared.

If you're a bar rescue fan And are on here to bash a bar you Have never been too then Screw off This bar supports live music of all kinds Which is a dead scene and bars like this keep punk, ska, reggae . . . metal alive. so don't believe a show that called us and put words in our mouth and then tries to charge us, this bar was going to be changed into a hipster bar with high end drinks and that is not us . . . if you support music in anyway you should realize that bars like this aren't made for everyone. [sic] thanks

I am not sure who or what the man is fighting with now. Social media posters? The rules of grammar? Punctuation? Himself? I mentioned earlier that 80 percent are worth the effort of constructive engagement, but 20 percent are just pointless time sucks. In which case, I'd argue that four walkaways from my show after more than two hundred episodes and counting is a respectable number. I am proud of my success rate, and grateful that I was able to help so many people over the years. Some conflicts were more bruising than others, but, with the rare exceptions mentioned above, these encounters always resulted in improved businesses and healthier communication with employees, business partners, family members, and customers.

It's just as important—in some ways maybe even more important—to make these calculations in our personal relationships. Most of us have known a person who always has a contrary opinion about everything. Maybe a relative, maybe a friend, maybe a co-worker. That individual who insists on disagreeing with you no matter how trivial the point, or how inappropriate the circumstances. You find yourself thinking, *Is it really worth my time and energy to disagree with every single thing she says—even though I get the feeling that's exactly what she wants?* Of course not.

You can rule these people out of the conflict equation by running them through a mental checklist. Before pilots take off, they use a worksheet to calculate factors like the weather, the length of their runway view, and other safety factors. At the end of that checklist, they quickly weigh whether or not to proceed. You can do something similar, calculating whether to proceed with a conflict by, say, rating your adversary's importance in your life on a scale of one to ten. If they rate a ten, you can ask yourself if the conflict helps or hurts the relationship in the long term, for example. This conflict calculation worksheet, or what some might call a gut check, could also rate opponents on their level of antagonism, the potential fallout of an engagement, or the likelihood of changing their minds. If you scan three or four of these factors in your brain, you may decide that, yes, indeed, this individual is important enough to you to be worth the effort of conflict and, though opinionated, is open enough to hear what you have to say.

We need to do the math and ask ourselves: What is the cost of walking away and what is the cost of conflict? Choose the one with the least cost. It can be a subjective personal thing for each instance: What will you lose without conflict, and what can you win? Again, some people are not worth the conflict. It is just the way they are wired. No one can change their minds, because they resist logic and debate, so it's better to avoid the raised blood pressure. Also, some topics are not approachable. Certainly, religious, political, and other deeply rooted beliefs can be impossible to even discuss, nonetheless change—so don't make the effort. You'll be the loser. Conflict cannot be won against minds that will not listen. Conflict is a tool, but as with all tools, it has a specific use for a specific purpose, and in some instances, it is *not* the right one to use.

Stoking False Fires

This is especially true in cases of fake conflict, or actions taken specifically to set up divisiveness and the problems that can cause. Engaging in fake conflict never leads to positive outcomes, and you should learn to recognize, disarm, and dismiss it. In other words, don't fall for it. People have used false conflict to stir up trouble and strife for centuries. It can be done on a macro level or a micro level—governments do it, businesses do it, people do it. It's happening as I write this. Keyboard warriors of all stripes are putting made-up or exaggerated stories onto Twitter, TikTok, and Instagram to further a biased narrative and create clickbait that goes viral, with lives and businesses damaged along the way.

In today's digital world, where social media has elevated conflict to fever-pitch levels, and where it can be used for both good and evil, we also need to be aware of fake news and other forms of misinformation that are specifically produced to create negative and destructive conflict. (In chapter 8, I will explain why social media is rarely the right forum for constructive engagement, and how to deflect these online skirmishes so that they don't blow up in the virtual echo chamber.)

We can also create false and damaging conflicts in our own minds. When I rescued Spirits on Bourbon, a bar in New Orleans, its owner, Brad Bohannan, believed his business was being negatively affected by a competitor. As a result, Brad focused all his energies on what his competitor was up to instead of his own business. He thought he was having a conflict with a business, but that conflict existed only in his own mind. The other business, the object of his rage and jealousy, was minding its own business, literally. When I began to challenge this, Brad and I had our own conflict. The more I pushed him on his own view of his business, the more open he became to reassessing his practices and behaviors. Brad was *forced* to reassess the real conflict that was holding him back—it wasn't a conflict with his competitor. It was his own inattention to what really mattered—his business.

After two days of intense evaluation, changes, training, and new products, Brad became excited with his business and started to forget about his imaginary conflict with the bar down the street. On our final day of filming, we walked down Bourbon Street together and stood in front of the competitor that had been Brad's focus. I asked him if the actions of this competitor mattered to his business. When Brad said no, my job was done.

Papa Bear Goes In

Using the power of conflict for good requires a level of discernment and honesty about your own motives and goals as much as the other party's. It's not something I enter into lightly, despite the fact that my media image, my brand, often seems combative. As a father, I struggled over whether to go there with the teachers and principal of my daughter's school. She and a classmate had worked hard on a science project. It was too good, one of her teachers decided, and she called the girls out in front of the entire fourth-grade class, falsely accusing and humiliating them, never once giving them the opportunity to defend themselves against the charge of cheating.

My daughter, a straight-A student and an honest kid full of integrity, burst into tears when she got home that night.

"Honey, what happened?" I asked her.

She was a little reluctant to tell me at first. Not because she thought for one moment I wouldn't take her side. She knew her daddy would step up for her, and then some. But a parent's intervention can have unintended consequences. It could change her teachers' attitudes toward her, and she would have to deal with these people for the next few years. I also knew she didn't want to be "that kid" whose parents fight her battles for her. It was a real dilemma for me. At the same time, I could not let this lie. Those two young ladies had been dealt a huge injustice that needed to be addressed firmly, adult to adult. After ruminating on it for a while, I asked myself: "How could I *not* show my daughter the true meaning and value of conflict by sticking up for her as a father?"

The next day, I arranged to meet with the principal, the teacher, and my daughter and her friend all in one room. I wanted the principal to hear both sides of the story, from student and teacher. Hearing them both, it was obvious the teacher had wrongly rushed to judgment, and the degrading manner in which he treated the girls was inexcusable. I went in hard, and the teacher sincerely apologized to my daughter and her classmate—the other girl who was unjustly accused. No one in that school messed with them again.

Many parents would tell their child to let it go. But that's exactly the wrong example to set. There are certain moments in life that test us as human beings, and we are either going to buckle or stick up for ourselves. If your conflict trigger point isn't the mistreatment of your child, then what's it gonna take?

That teachable moment stayed with my daughter, who is now all grown up and a parent herself. She's never been afraid to go there. She is a successful adult because she understands that constructive, positive conflict helps create an environment in which disputes can be settled at lower levels. She gets why settling small disputes as they occur is better than letting them escalate. Throughout her life, she's empowered herself through constructive conflict.

But, in order to reach this promised land, we first have to accept that conflict is a natural part of life and, more importantly, we must learn how to engage in conflict fairly and honestly. Now that you have the tools to choose the right battles, recognizing where conflict *is* authentic and appropriate, in the following chapter I am going to teach you the rules of engagement. Even the most violent blood sports have codes of conduct, and wars have combat codes. Once you decide to step into that arena, you must fight fair.

Taffer Toolkit Takeaways

1. *Use your conflict calculator.* Determine whether the person you are thinking about entering into the arena with is a worthy adversary. If you've known this individual for a while, think back on their past interactions with others. Does he fight fair? Is she capable of listening?

2. *Figure out your goal.* Can the issue be resolved through other strategies besides direct confrontation? Does a

discussion that could get angry and heated, potentially damaging long-term relationships, further an important goal? What's the bigger picture?

3. *Learn to recognize fake conflict.* Is someone just stirring the pot to get attention or further their own agenda? Is it in your own head? Have you created an external conflict where none exists to avoid facing your own failings?

4

THE RULES OF ENGAGEMENT

Fight the good fight: clean and fair.

I n Season Four of *Bar Rescue*, I traveled to Oregon to help out the Six Point Inn, a family-owned bar located in a small blue-collar neighborhood of St. Johns in northern Portland. Their Over Easy Bar & Breakfast was one of just a handful of bars in its neighborhood when it first opened its doors in 2009. But then the owner, Oleg Pilipenko, decided to shift his focus to opening other businesses, and left his inexperienced stepdaughter, Sunny, in control of the bar's daily operations. Sunny's resentment with Oleg created a toxic work environment, which led to declining staff morale and chasing customers away. With an absent owner and a crumbling family relationship, Six Point Inn began to fail, leaving the bar with $1 million in debt.

I quickly learned that the failing business was the symptom of a much deeper problem, which is usually the case. The family dysfunction—stepfather's and stepdaughter's failure to communicate in a healthy way with each other—was at the root of it all. I had to get the two owners talking to each other honestly and openly, allowing Oleg to express his frustrations, and Sunny to explain her resentment. But first, I had to set the rules of engagement.

The Golden Rule—"do unto others"—is the key to constructive conflict. Oleg and Sunny had to stop talking past each other. They had to stop relitigating past grievances with every argument and focus on the issue at hand. Each had to let the other speak their mind without fear of being drowned out or dismissed. My Taffer Toolkit rules of engagement are based on respect—the basis of any civil discourse. Some are common courtesy; all are common sense.

Respect Your Adversary

You don't have to look far to find these rules of engagement. They can be found everywhere from college debating societies to Senate and congressional hearing committees in our nation's capital, although lately it may seem like those folks have thrown out their rule books. Law students must learn the ground rules of civil discourse before they can even think about setting foot in a US courtroom. One of the first things they learn is that "it's not the loudest voice that prevails"[1] in the courtroom. Instead, the best adversarial approach is grounded in reason and evidence that are presented according to strict rules of decorum. Asking questions of each side is integral to the process. Even when you are on opposing sides, you are working together to reach the truth.

Again, these are human beings on the other side of the engagement. Going into a conflict with the mindset that you will respect your opponent has the additional benefit of reducing the volume and intensity and creates the environment in which you can have a real exchange of thoughts and ideas. If your adversary isn't hung up on how he's perceived (or, more accurately, how he perceives he's perceived), then you have bypassed needless posturing and one-upmanship and engaged in dialogue that is honest and meaningful. So make sure you do not talk down or diminish your adversary. Pointing out flaws or mistakes in facts and reasoning is critical to resolving conflict; attacking the person is not.

And I cannot emphasize enough the importance of finding common ground. That small effort goes a long way toward opening up the ears of your adversary, which is the whole point. As you present your argument, use specific examples that your opponent can relate to. Make your case in terms your opponent can understand. What you are really doing is looking for ways to build bonds that come from acknowledging shared experiences. In *Marriage Rescue*, when I talk to couples locked in conflict over the future of their marriage, I often mention both of my marriages—my first failed marriage and my wildly successful twenty-two-year-and-counting second marriage. I know what they are going through because I've been there too. This approach allows us to agree upon common struggles, and a meaningful dialogue emerges as the partners also begin to see their common ground.

Attack Policies, Not Politicians

One of the best examples of someone who engages in conflict the right way is Howard Schultz, former CEO of Starbucks. Whatever one's politics, he is undeniably a class act in the way he approaches his adversaries. He makes his case by focusing on the actions, policies, or decisions, not the character of the individual. It's never personal.

The coffee chain has often been found at the center of various culture wars. Schultz and, by association, Starbucks became the target of many conservatives over things like its pro-immigration stance, former president Donald Trump's refugee policy, gun rights, race in America, and LGBTQ rights. Schultz was even willing to go public on positions that would not be popular with either party, like taking on the national debt. But when you look back at Schultz's statements, notice he stayed above the fray. It was always about policies, not politicians; actions, not tweets. In response to the Trump administration's temporary bar against people seeking refugee status in the United States, for example, Starbucks pledged to hire ten thousand refugees over five years. While mindful not to alienate half the country, Schultz stood up for his core beliefs, and the values of his company, through levelheaded engagement.[2]

None of Schultz's positions on the issues have hurt Starbucks's revenues. If anything, taking principled stances and engaging in civil discourse have enhanced the company's brand by differentiating it from the average cup of coffee.

Following rules of engagement, fighting the fair fight, ensures a positive outcome. Conflict doesn't necessarily have to lead to collateral damage to your relationships or reputation. As long as you remember that there is a human being on the other side of your dispute, the greater the chance you will be heard by your opponent the right way, and hopefully change hearts and minds. It is a conscious, intentional, and civil approach to engagement that requires you to get out of your own head by doing the following:

- Practice self-awareness. Ask yourself: How am I reacting and responding when the other party speaks? Am I looking at my adversary? Is the person I am standing in the ring with receiving my full attention? Am I talking over or interrupting this person?

- Give your adversary a chance to respond. This is supposed to be a dialogue, not a hectoring speech.

- Ask questions. Don't assume you know what your adversary means. Ask clarifying follow-up questions. You will strengthen your argument when you better understand where your opponent is coming from.

- Search for common ground; find some type of connection. This is key. Though you may strongly disagree with your opponent on the issue you are discussing, this is not an evil person. Pick an undebatable fact (like the weather). Make a point of finding where you *can* agree to indicate the possibility of coming closer together in your opinions.

- Don't be rude! No eye rolls or impatient sighs. No demeaning comments. Maintain a level of respect, then gain the advantage with facts, logic, and passion. You'll never win with a pissy attitude.

- Understand the difference between facts and opinions.

- Always focus on the present issue. Don't use your time in the ring to relitigate every little thing that this person did to annoy you. Get some traction on the most pressing problem; let go of the small stuff, get to the root of the problem, and think big picture.

Of course, by rules of engagement, I do not mean there's only one correct approach to constructive conflict. Depending on the setting, the issue, or the temperament of your adversary, you might want to go in hot, or broach the subject gently, nailing them with facts in a calm tone. You can take people down to build them back up again, as I often do on *Bar Rescue*, but the one thing I never do is seek to destroy. I attack actions, not someone's identity, humanity, or appearance. Purposeful conflict should never be personal. Viciousness has no place in the Taffer Toolkit.

Art of the Deal

Full disclosure: I shared a similar negotiation style with former president Donald Trump, at least before he got into the White House. Some dealmakers come in soft then push and push in the final stages of negotiation, leaving a bit of tension on the table at the start of the relationship. But we go in hard. I build throwaways into the negotiation terms, which appear like concessions toward the end, so when the deal is signed, it allows the business relationship to start on better footing. But that is where the commonalities of our negotiation/conflict styles end.

Somehow President Trump lost his negotiation chops along the way. Now he seems to do conflict for conflict's sake and doesn't know when to quit. He robs people of their dignity with cruel barbs and nonstop insults, like the schoolyard bully. During his campaigns and presidency, when someone upset him, he tweeted about their physical appearance, their personal habits, their intelligence, or their perceived lack of success. His nasty, sexist remarks about women made me wince. People have called him a "counterpuncher," but I disagree. There's no give-and-take. He just squishes people.

Plenty of voters supported him, but he undermined himself by diminishing the politicians in D.C. who might otherwise have helped him along the way. If you call someone a fool before you start, no one will want to engage with you. Trump experienced that kind of isolation at the end of his term, as did New York Governor Andrew Cuomo, who took the same scorched-earth approach to anyone even remotely critical of his policies and actions.

Trump is a great example of wasted conflict. Conflict for its own sake is an ineffective strategy in any arena. As a leader, Trump's aggression undermined his effectiveness. No rules of engagement for this guy. It never occurred to him that it was beneath the office of the president to fight every trivial battle, from getting into the weeds with NASCAR driver Bubba Wallace over allegations of a noose hanging by his garage door to Arnold Schwarzenegger's ratings as host of *The New Celebrity Apprentice*. One of his worst tweets was about MSNBC personality Mika Brzezinski and her husband, Joe Scarborough:

> I heard poorly rated @Morning_Joe speaks badly of me (don't watch anymore). Then how come low I.Q. Crazy Mika, along with Psycho Joe, came to Mar-a-Lago 3 nights in a row

around New Year's Eve, and insisted on joining me. She was bleeding badly from a face-lift. I said no!

It was probably one of the crudest personal attacks of Trump's presidency. It was a textbook example of how not to engage in constructive conflict.

Mika lashed back:

Let's say someone came into NBC and took over NBC and started tweeting wildly about people's appearances, bullying people, talking about people in the competition, lying every day, undermining his managers, throwing them under the— that person would be thrown out. It's just not normal behavior. In fact, there would be concern that perhaps the person who runs the company is out of his mind.

She was absolutely right. Trump may have been stung by earlier comments the TV couple had made about his presidency, but he lost more points when he climbed down into the mud pit and started slinging dirt. When you fight with someone on every petty thing, it's not healthy engagement. It's just constant antagonism that prevents future communication. No one is going to hear you on what really matters when you behave like a mad dog. No one is going to engage with you in a healthy, constructive way if they know you're going to humiliate them at the slightest provocation.

A Bit o' Blarney

Decades ago, our political leaders on both sides of the aisle dealt with conflict on a level that was professional, not personal. Former Democratic House Speaker Tip O'Neill and Ronald Reagan disagreed with each other vehemently on most issues. They were sworn enemies, with the Speaker doing everything he could to block Reagan's tax cuts and deregulations. But, about a year and a half into his first term, when the country was facing a major budget deficit and the markets were getting jittery, Reagan realized he needed O'Neill's support to pass through legislation that would stabilize the economy. So he invited his foe to the White House for a meeting, breaking the ice with his fellow Irish American by telling a dirty Irish joke.

It was a good start, because they spent the next several months talking despite their differences, until they were able to draft the Tax Equity and Fiscal Responsibility Act of 1982, set up a bipartisan committee on social security, and straighten out the country's public retirement system. All because the two men were able to find that tiny sliver of common ground.

Whether they became the best of friends is debatable. But rumor has it that O'Neill was the first, outside of family members, to visit Reagan in the hospital after he was shot. Reagan and O'Neill were also known to share a few beers after a day of exchanging sharp political barbs. The point is, they kept talking and getting important legislation passed. And they shared more Irish jokes and plenty of mutual affection at O'Neill's retirement bash on St. Patrick's Day in 1986.

"He [Reagan] calls me up and says, 'It's after six o'clock—do we still have to be mad?" O'Neill told the crowd at the party. "So we sit down and tell a few Irish lies."

Reagan had them roaring when he told everyone O'Neill had invited him to the event because he wanted someone who had actually known St. Patrick.

"It's true, I did know St. Patrick, Tip. We both changed parties about the same time."[3]

I miss those days when we could put aside our differences and connect purely as human beings. We get rare glimpses. Whenever

Michelle Obama and former president George W. Bush are seated near each other at an event, Bush sneaks her a candy. Politically, they are opposites, but they chat like old friends. This type of behavior among opposites and rivals was the norm for hundreds of years. After a church, the next thing to be built in Washington, D.C., was likely a bar. Our first leaders, after hours of intense arguing over the laws or our young nation, would wash away that day's acrimony with pints of beer, drams of whiskey, and glasses of wine. They'd joke or commiserate with each other and, as impossible as it seemed to reach a deal earlier in the day, suddenly find themselves able to concede on those last stubborn points with a mutual slap on the back or shoulder squeeze.

On the Record

Building that human connection was my go-to tactic when I learned I would be doing a sit-down interview with Donald Trump at the Trump International Hotel in Las Vegas just weeks before the 2020 election. To be clear, I wasn't interested in endorsing either of the presidential candidates. Politics was not what led to this conversation so much as my concern over the struggles faced by my industry in the previous months. My goal was to get the policies of both men on the record for the hospitality industry—vital in every state to be sure, but the absolute lifeblood of the Nevada economy. In fact, I wanted to give them equal airtime, so I reached out to Joe Biden's campaign three times for a similar conversation but received no response. Through all the campaign noise, there'd been little to no discussion about policies that would impact the thousands of mom-and-pops who were struggling to keep the lights on. I felt a sense of urgency because, across the board, the restaurant industry had lost more jobs and revenue than any industry in America.

To make this podcast interview happen, I enlisted the help of some friends in the media to make the pitch.

"No one really knows your policies for the industry," I reminded them. "This will be a chance for the candidate to win over the union workers and small business owners of Nevada—votes that could really count."

It was supposed to be a Skype call, but I was stunned to learn that President Trump was not only willing, but eager to meet with me in person. They even allowed us to produce and own our content, with no editing rights. In fact, Trump's team was gracious and remarkably transparent. I got all the time I needed from him and then some. But what I did not want was for the president to hijack my platform to talk about impeachment, or Hunter Biden's laptop, or any of the other distracting stories of the moment. I knew he wasn't fond of being interrupted and could go down a rabbit hole if he was so inclined. But this was about getting some real commitment to my industry at a time when it was struggling and businesses were closing by the thousands due to COVID restrictions. What would be his promise to them to get one of the nation's biggest block of employers back on track?

Technically, we weren't exactly engaged in a conflict. I already had a sense that we'd be on the same side of the issue. But I was nervous because I knew how hard he could push back if he was irked in some way. I had my own agenda I was determined to stick to, so I prepared as if I were going into battle because, based on his history, there was every chance the guy could get combative. I did extensive research going into the interview, so I had plenty of facts to call upon if necessary. I worked for hours on my six-minute interview with President Donald Trump. It might have looked like a casual conversation, but I scanned all the congressional acts that pertained to our topic—thousands of pages. I also watched past interviews to see how best to steer the conversation (preferably away from the subject of House Speaker Nancy Pelosi). My end goal was to have certain questions answered. It was a purpose-driven, premeditated engagement and absolutely nothing was left to chance. The more information you have, the less need there is to make noise and divert attention away from what matters.

I started with the common ground tactic and reminded him that he was one of us. (Most of his career was spent building and running hotels, resorts, and casinos.) I disarmed Trump right away by making him feel a sense of camaraderie with me. Putting him at ease and acknowledging his expertise in my industry enabled him to be his most articulate, best self. I allowed him to speak but took control of the narrative, getting him back on course with each question and interjection, ignoring what wasn't relevant and repeating what he said back to him when it was an idea I wanted to highlight and explore.

Overall, I was impressed by the president's grasp of the facts. He displayed a deep and thorough knowledge not just of my industry, but of the details of the many loan and grant programs implemented during the COVID pandemic. The facts he could spit out surprised me. He had exceptional recall of the data. He made eye contact with me, spoke empathetically about the small business owners who were suffering, and got specific about what stimulus programs and aid he was willing to throw his weight behind should he get reelected.

First, he talked about broadening the employee retention tax credit, to help our business owners keep their staff on the payroll. Second, he promised to extend a PPP program to cover debt. Third— and this was huge—he committed to reintroducing the business lunch tax credit. These business meal write-offs would attract more high-paying diners and be a much-needed boost to revenues. Finally, he committed to a domestic-travel incentive program, which could be a lifeline to destinations like Las Vegas and Miami, as well as business markets like New York and Los Angeles.

There were moments when the president veered, but I employed a combination of eye contact and encouraging nods as I listened for relevant phrases that would give me the opportunity to bring him back into the present moment and the topic at hand—my struggling industry—using many of the same methods I employ on my show, minus the yelling. By the end of the conversation, it struck me how bright Donald Trump is in some ways, yet weak when it comes to understanding humanity. Having studied the man's pugilistic style for years, I was able to employ the sharpest tools in my toolkit to check off my wish list while maintaining a cordial, constructive engagement. At least for that particular interview, he showed up as the leader I would have liked him to be—someone who was looking out for the little guy.

It saddened me when, post-election, Trump eclipsed that side of his character and intellect by encouraging an angry crowd of supporters to go to the Capitol and protest the electoral vote. He was baiting everyone who wouldn't go along with his desire to overturn the results—even his own loyal vice president. He sowed discord, promoting disruption because he couldn't accept that that battle had already been lost, like a toddler having an epic meltdown. It was more wasted conflict that not only deluded and destroyed the lives of a multitude of his staunchest supporters, it was a slap in the face of our Constitution.

Trump's lack of graciousness and failure to be circumspect violated every rule of healthy engagement, tarnishing the Republican brand. That's exactly the kind of extreme that can happen when months and years go by without productive dialogue to resolve differences, or at least come to a mutual understanding over them. You self-destruct.

True Victory

Conflict is not necessarily about winning. If all you are focused on is scoring that next point and demolishing your opponent, you're in it for the wrong reasons. Healthy, constructive engagement is about helping people wake up and see that something needs to be fixed. It's about raising awareness and promoting positive change. It's about moving that needle on the dial forward, if even by a millimeter. The person on the opposite side may walk away feeling they've won the day, but as long as you put your best case out there and conducted yourself with class, you've scored the truest victory. You can walk away with your head held high. And you never know, you may have planted a subtle seed of doubt in your opponent's mind. Outside the arena, as this individual reflects back on the exchange, your words may have ignited an internal conflict that chips away at that sense of righteousness. Maybe over time this person will be better able to receive a different perspective. If not, at least you were courageous enough to try.

Dr. Ian Smith, whom you met in chapter 1, doesn't go into battle with the end goal of proving he is right. For him, conflict is a tool for saving the lives of his patients. While many trust him and take his advice at face value, he gets a surprising amount of pushback.

"I don't know, Doc, I've been eating this way for years and there's nothing wrong with me," one patient told him.

"My grandmother smoked until she was ninety-five," said another.

Rather than react to the absurdity of these statements, Ian tries to understand how things appear from their perspective.

"First, I acknowledge where they are and why they feel the way they do," Ian told me. "Grandma may be an anomaly, an odd plot on a graph, but, to that person, she is a real data point, so I try to turn the lens a bit rather than come in straightaway with my opposite viewpoint."

Shucking the Oyster

While some respond well to a more dogmatic, firm approach, Ian knows the cause is lost when the patient's defensive walls go up.

"You have to read the temperature and understand the person you are working with. You have to win them over to your side somehow."

He looks for that small opening, like the weak spot between the shells of an oyster before you shuck it.

"Find the 'in' in whatever discussion it is," Ian explained. "Figure out how they truly feel about something. Everyone has a crack or a crevice somewhere, and your job is to find it. It won't necessarily be in the first conversation, but if you are creative and persistent, you will find that emotional opening."

Ian uses various engagement techniques depending on the disposition of his patient. One that rarely fails is transparency. Rather than approach someone as the expert who knows all, for example, he'll admit when he doesn't know something. Whether the individuals he's treating intend to or not, they'll often mirror Ian's transparency and begin to open up. They'll begin to trust him more as he reveals that he, too, is a work in progress. To build trust, Ian will use language like, "That's not my area of knowledge, but guess what, I'm going to find out for you." He gives them a sense that he's working *with* them toward their well-being. They say to themselves, "Okay, this guy doesn't think he's perfect." In their minds, he's leveled the playing field, enabling a real dialogue.

"Talking down to someone from a pedestal will either fuel resentment or intimidate them into silence, which ends the engagement before it can even begin. So you try to be more approachable. You make them feel like you are someone they can talk to."

One of Ian's toughest nuts to crack was on his show *Celebrity Fit Club*. A celebrity "just wasn't there." She didn't believe in the program, she was constantly pushing back, and her negativity was infecting the rest of the participants. He couldn't figure out why she agreed to be on the show if she was adopting this attitude, but rather than trying to lecture or shame her into changing her behavior, he tapped around to figure out the source of this bad energy.

It turned out that being on the show wasn't the young woman's idea. She was overweight, but not severely so, and had yet to see any major health consequences of her eating habits and lifestyle choices. She was convinced her weight gain was "much ado about nothing."

Having gently probed enough to understand where she was coming from, Ian realized the tough love approach would fail. It wasn't simply a matter of saying, "Hey, you need to lose twenty-five pounds to get to a healthy BMI." He needed to make his case as if he were a lawyer in a courtroom, with logic, facts, and data to get her on the right path. He plotted out her weight gain over the previous few years on a timeline, charting out where she would be in ten years if she didn't change her ways.

"Based on your historical pattern, you'll be at risk for type 2 diabetes, kidney disease, and heart disease," he told her.

She didn't like what she heard, but she had nothing to say in her own defense. The evidence was right in front of her face. The facts disarmed her. As she was downloading this harsh reality, he hit her with this question:

"Tell me something: If you don't think this is a problem, why did you come here?"

She was put on the spot, but in a good way, because it got her to think more deeply about what she wanted out of the whole experience.

"It was an interesting moment for her because she either had to admit that she was just on the show for the money, which would not have been a good look, or that she wanted to get help. She finally admitted that she wanted to improve her life, and that was my opening. From that point on, I could be the guy to help her find ways to improve her life. Her attitude did a one-eighty. She started enjoying the program and seeing results."

Over the years, Ian has become an expert at finding the opening that will allow for constructive conflict. He's come to realize that not every individual on the other side of the engagement will react in exactly the same way. For some, it might be a question along the lines of, "Do you want to live to see your grandchild walk across that stage and get that diploma?" For others, it might be an appeal to their self-esteem. "Do you want to look and feel good in that formfitting designer dress?" But the conversation doesn't even start until he's broken through and made that human-to-human connection. The tough love can't happen until he establishes a level of trust and mutual respect.

Father of the Year

On *Bar Rescue*, the root cause of the issue is almost always some kind of emotional dysfunction with the owner and, by extension, the owner's family, as it's often the case in small businesses that husbands, wives, children, parents, and siblings are involved in the operations. I'm the guy who can come in and get them to confront issues in their lives that they tiptoe around, knowing they have to go home at the end of the night with this person. But it's not just about banging heads together. It's an art.

There was a lot to unravel at the Game Time Sports Grill in Arlington, Tennessee. This Season Six episode felt more like a family therapy session than a professional bar makeover. Bryan Cochran, a retired construction worker, had always wanted to own a sports bar, so he and his wife, Teresa, invested their retirement savings in a location about thirty miles east of Memphis that was lacking area bars and restaurants. At first, the customers came in a steady stream and revenues were solid. But they couldn't sustain their popularity because they lacked the experience—an all-too-common story.

Ticket times were slow on food that was not worth the wait. The kitchen was a whole other story—one of the worst I'd seen. The people preparing food weren't wearing gloves and the area was filthy, creating extreme risk for cross contamination. There was black mold everywhere and the freezer was broken. The health department would have shut them down if they'd gotten within a hundred yards of the place. The bar and waitstaff did their best, but they were overwhelmed and undertrained.

Bryan and Teresa soon ran into deep debt. To avoid losing the premises to bankruptcy, they put the establishment, and the $250,000 debt they'd accrued, into their grown son Cody's name. Cody was forced to choose between his parents and his dream of becoming an air traffic controller. He chose his parents and stepped up to run the bar that had quickly become an albatross around his neck. His first child was due in six weeks at the time of our taping, and the losses were piling up. The bar was about to break three generations of a family.

At the beginning of each episode, I do a recon. My production team installs spy cameras throughout the bar, and I park somewhere discreet near the premise and monitor what's happening in real time alongside my team of experts. I sat horrified as a drunken Dad sat at the bar, drinking and giving away shots to female customers as he berated his son and his staff. Fed up, Teresa dragged him out back to scold him about his inappropriate behavior, accusing him of drinking what little profits the bar had, and Bryan shoved past her as he angrily stumbled back inside.

I'd seen enough. You don't get physical on my watch, so I stepped in and confronted Bryan with his behavior. I rolled the tape on my tablet, which, by the way, is perfectly fine under my rules of engagement. Use all the technology you want to confront someone with the truth. Go ahead and press record on your phone! Make denial impossible.

I gave Bryan hell. I warned him that if he touched one liquor bottle while I was there, I would walk. I reminded him that he put this huge burden on his only son just as his first grandchild was about to be born. The poor kid was sinking. Meanwhile, Dad sat there at the bar, selfishly drinking the profits away and watching as Cody and Teresa worked hard to try to salvage the business. Father of the Year tried to defend himself and deny what I saw with my own eyes, so I rubbed his nose in what he'd done to his kid, disrespecting Cody and making him feel like he was always having to push a rock up a hill.

"Your son is ashamed that you're his father!" I told him.

That got him. But as soon as Dad broke down and cried, Mom put her arms around him.

"Don't hug him so quickly, Teresa. Make him prove it! You're an enabler and if you keep hugging him in failure, he has no reason to change!"

I told Cody to take charge and send his father home, which he did. Cody was a bright and capable guy whose confidence was being undermined by the father who resented the fact that he was no longer the boss. Cody had what I call the "broken syndrome," with hunched-over shoulders and an unwillingness to speak his mind. I wanted this father-to-be to stand up straight, take charge, and assert himself. It's not an easy thing to do under the shadow of an alpha male father, but Cody had to put his own wife and child first. He had to take ownership of the bar for the sake of his future or bring a baby into this world under the cloud of debt, unable to provide his young family with all the things they needed and deserved. I knew that before we could get the operations of the bar right, Cody and Bryan's relationship had to be healed.

The next day, a sober and contrite Bryan showed up. Now was my opportunity to break down the barriers between these family members and restore what used to be a healthy dynamic before the money problems took over. I'd finally gotten to the bottom of what was making Bryan behave like such an asshole—guilt. He couldn't bring himself to face up to the situation he'd gotten his son into. He knew he had failed Cody and himself, and he was projecting all that self-loathing onto everyone around him, including his wife. But I made Bryan see that this was his opportunity to lend support and get them all out of this mess.

"I gotta fix the two of you," I told Bryan and Cody. "Bryan, Cody is scared to open up to you. You've fallen into a pattern in your relationship where it's easier to say the negative than speak the positive."

I wasn't trying to go for the jugular in this conversation. I could see that Bryan had already reached a turning point. He wanted to make things right. And Cody was more willing to be open about where everything stood in the business.

"Does your son not deserve one hundred percent commitment to his success?" I asked Bryan, gently this time.

"I promise to give him support," he told me, tears welling up in his eyes. "From now on I have his back."

For the rest of the episode, Bryan did step up. During the stress test, when we invite a hundred or so customers in to fill up the bar and put in a maximum number of drink and food orders, Bryan proved himself extremely capable behind the bar and didn't touch a drop of alcohol. Although there were still a lot of operational challenges to address, the repaired relationship made it possible. Bryan's support of Cody gave Cody the confidence to be more commanding and present as an owner.

The establishment's name was changed to Legacy Bar & Grill in honor of the grandchild it will be passed on to, Cody's business became a local favorite among the hip and affluent crowd of young Memphis suburbanites. And the last time I checked the family still worked well together. But it could not have happened without a highly strategic approach to confrontation.

I came in hot, because Bryan needed to wake up and see what he was doing to himself and his family, but I had to do it in such a way that the whole family wouldn't turn on me and rush to his defense. I attacked his actions, not who he was as a man. I got specific about what he was doing and how it was hurting the business, his relationships, and the future of his grandchild. When I saw the sincere remorse in his eyes and heard the resolve in his voice to do better, there was no point in continuing to hit him over the head repeatedly. I went after him on the fundamentals of self-respect and love for his family. After taking him down, I could build him back up.

Once I was able to gain his trust, everything changed. My intentions coming into that scenario were no longer feared. I was no longer a threat; I was an ally. Now I could make him part of the process—the solution, not the problem. Through strategic confrontation, I became the guy who could help him rebuild that key relationship with his son and teach him how he could best step up and support him. But I had to balance my approach, employing the rules of engagement to ensure that Bryan felt like more of a stakeholder than a guy being scolded, belittled, or dictated to in front of his family and former staff.

Play It Back

There is a whole science to how you can manage a conflict to keep the flow of communication and enable a more constructive engagement. The Space Medicine Innovations Lab at Dartmouth College has developed approaches based on the understanding that we often put our own meaning onto what someone is actually saying and misinterpret intentions. There are certain triggers that can lead to a cascade of misunderstanding, anger, and resentment that takes an engagement completely off the rails.

"People can take offense at things where none was intended," explains Jay Buckey, whom you met in Chapter One. "The same set of facts can be interpreted in so many different ways. That's why it's important to remember how easy it is to misunderstand the meanings of what is said and done."

Dr. Buckey and his team at Dartmouth have developed the self-guided PATH program, which teaches people how to manage the cycle of conflict and recognize points where it's gotten out of control.[4] The gist of it is this: When an argument seems to spiral and you're not sure exactly how you got there, it's time to pump the brakes. People are not responding objectively to what is being said so much as responding to the meaning they put on it. Instead of reacting, take a minute to try to understand what is actually being said by repeating it back to that person.

"So when you said X, Y, Z just now, did you mean A, B, C?"

The PATH program reenacts a couple of astronauts in space getting on each other's nerves as they go through a checklist. Another more common real-world example might be a colleague telling you, "This conference room is a mess." You might take that statement of fact to mean she thinks you are a slob, so you get angry, thinking your colleague is a judgmental, passive-aggressive nudge. But you would save yourself a world of pain by taking a minute to calmly repeat her words back to her, to make sure not only that you understood her correctly, but that she feels she's being heard.

"When you said that the conference room is a mess, I took away that you think I am not taking proper care of this place." Maybe that was what she meant to say. But there is a good chance it was just intended as a casual observation. By repeating her words back to her, you are giving her a chance to clarify so that you can deescalate the conflict and allow the discussion to move forward. The engagement may still get heated, but at least you will clear the way to focus on the real points of contention.

I'll give you several more techniques for engagement in the coming chapters, but my one golden rule boils down to this: Never forget your adversary's humanity. When you treat someone with respect, when you give them their dignity, the chances are greater that what you have to say will be received.

Within that larger framework, consider the person and the circumstances within the conflict. If it's a workplace disagreement and you have to show up the next day to face the same people, you might want to dial down the passion. If it's a conflict with friends, acquaintances, or neighbors, you may decide to make a different calculation. You can leave it on the floor if you're okay with some fallout. Maybe you don't need to invite the family across the street to your next barbecue if it's more important to you that they curb their dog instead of letting him pee on your lawn. But if it's a family conflict, consider these wise words from the good Dr. Ian:

"When you love somebody, the more you should be willing to engage in conflict, particularly with family. But keep a live tracking to determine if it's going in the right or wrong direction, because there is no conflict big enough to be worth losing that kind of relationship."

Think about that at your next Thanksgiving dinner.

Taffer Toolkit Takeaways

1. *Be relatable.* Talking down to someone from a pedestal will either fuel resentment or intimidate them into silence, which ends the engagement before it can even begin.

2. *Find the "in."* Whatever the discussion is, try to read the temperature and understand the person you are working with.

3. *Play it back.* The same set of facts can be interpreted in so many different ways. That's why it's important to remember how easy it is to misunderstand the meanings of what is said and done.

4. *Consider the person and the circumstances within the conflict.* If it's a workplace disagreement and you must show up the next day to face the same people, dial down the passion.

5. *Research the rules of engagement from other institutions,* such as "The Principles of Discourse," introduced by a former college president during a convocation speech and long since used at Hampshire College in Amherst, Massachusetts, to provide students, faculty, and staff with a road map for handling disagreements respectfully.

6. *Conflict is not necessarily about winning.* If all you are focused on is scoring that next point, you're in it for the wrong reasons. True victory can be something as small as planting a mustard seed. Give them a new idea to think about, then sit back and watch it grow.

7. *Never forget your adversary's humanity.* When you treat someone with respect, when you give them their dignity, the chances are greater that what you have to say will be received. It's my golden rule.

5

DO YOUR HOMEWORK

Even when you can't control the timing of a confrontation, you know it's coming. So be prepared.

'm a big mouth. I know. I get loud with people. I get in their faces. Some come right out and say it . . . Taffer is obnoxious. If you've seen me in action on *Bar Rescue*, you might be inclined to agree. What you see, though, isn't always what you get. When I confront bar owners or warring couples, I have done so only after I have investigated the situation. I send in my undercover teams to do research so that I can study the players and their plays. I sit in my car, parked discreetly outside, observing how they conduct business through a livestream video feed from cameras placed throughout their establishment, so that I can assess the situation with my own eyes. It's only after I have the facts that I take action. Trust me, it may *look* like I'm foaming at the mouth, but there is *always* a method to my (perceived) madness.

One of the surest paths to engaging in unproductive conflict is taking action based on untested or unproven assumptions. Before you begin a discussion that may escalate into something more serious, know what you know—and what you don't know—about the situation.

Imagine, for example, you have a a nine-to-five office job. You get up early each morning to make the train, bleary-eyed from a poor night's rest, but what choice do you have? It's at least an hour-long commute on a good day. By mid-afternoon you get drowsy, but you push through, drinking the stale coffee, doing your best to stay alert and productive until it's time to punch out, fight the traffic, and get home. So it drives you crazy that your co-worker leaves five minutes early every day; this habitual skipping out has become a sore point, and now you can't even bring yourself to say good morning to the guy. The atmosphere around your cubicles is frosty. Although you don't like to think of yourself as a tattletale, you're about to tell the boss. That'll fix Mr. End His Day Before It's Over.

Then one day your wife drops you off at work a little early. You head for your cubicle, and there is your co-worker clearly immersed in his work. His day obviously started before you arrived. Without thinking, you blurt out, "What are you doing here?" Your colleague replies, "Because I've had to leave early ever since the bus schedule changed, I've been coming in early to make up the time. Hadn't you noticed? My supervisor okayed it." Well, no, you hadn't. The "conflict" that you perceived because you didn't know all of the circumstances suddenly dissipates. Who's the asshole now?

Save yourself a world of hurt by taking a moment—or longer—to consider what you think you know and the reasons you see conflict brewing, to determine if they are truly based in fact and not assumptions. Take that time to get your ducks in a row and make sure you have gathered all the necessary facts and evidence by doing the following:

- Make sure your information is accurate and complete. Do your research!

- Use only information relevant to the conflict—the everything-but-the-kitchen-sink approach is not helpful.

- Target your research by imagining what information you would use if you were on the other side of the debate, then gather enough evidence to shoot those points down!

- Don't get thrown when your adversary rattles off statistics. Yogi Berra once said, "If you torture numbers enough, they will tell you anything." If you don't know where they were sourced or if they are even true, don't allow yourself to be distracted. Instead, steer the discussion back to the information you know to be solid.

- Double-check. Nothing derails an argument faster than a simple check of facts. Again, make sure yours are correct.

Seniors Gone Wild

Property manager Ketty Urbay does all of the above.

Growing up the eldest child in a large and boisterous Cuban American family, she got drawn into every conflict as the family peacemaker. Her mother and father often squabbled and, from a young age, Ketty felt the burden of stepping in to solve everyone else's problems, be they her parents' marital woes, sibling rivalries, or dramas among school friends. So it's hardly surprising that she grew up to found her own property management company in South Florida, where contentious condo board meetings are just another Tuesday.

"These meetings can get crazy," Ketty shared with me. "Condos are like businesses, with budgets and complicated governance laws, and little in the way of infrastructure to help board members run things correctly. They are volunteers who think they know what they're doing, but to them it's like a game of monopoly. All these egos, combined with lack of experience, can create a big mess."

One such mess occurred at a large 55+ community in a Miami suburb that was having renovation work done to meet the city's requirements for recertification. It was such a contentious problem that at least fifty of the two hundred owners turned up for the meeting, cramming the community room, the majority of whom were eighty years or older. As Ketty's business partners went around getting people to sign in for the meeting, one elderly woman, Agnes, refused to relinquish the clipboard. Agnes was tiny, less than a hundred pounds soaking wet, but she had a fierce grip and began shrieking when someone attempted to pry it from her grasp. Before the meeting could even begin, all hell broke loose, and the other owners, thinking Agnes was being physically attacked, came lunging toward the table. Another octogenarian, this one an imposing six foot three, lifted up her wooden cane and started swinging it at Ketty and her team. The situation got so out of hand that she had to call the police.

"I was horrified at the time, but in hindsight I guess it was pretty funny, like Seniors Gone Wild," Ketty jokes.

One little old lady even lay on the ground with her arms and legs folded, telling the officers, "Go ahead, arrest me! Jail will be better than this hellhole!"

Even after that conflict, Ketty stayed with the client for eight years, helping them to resolve the building issues in question, and many more. Experience taught her that no matter how nutty these condo associations can get, when she arms herself with information, drilling down for every possible angle and data point, she prevails. There is little a board president can throw at her that she hasn't already seen or heard about, whether it's getting bids for a roof contractor, running a highly contested board election, or collecting maintenance fees that are months in arrears.

"I put a lot of hours into my reports. The work is already being done to that level of detail because I approach everything as if it were my money, my home, my building. I ask a lot of questions and examine every angle. I read every email and know the numbers front and back, so I am never caught with my pants down."

Emotional Inventory

But, through the years, Ketty began to realize that preparing for these encounters wasn't just about knowing the facts. She'd reached a point of burnout, reacting more emotionally to conflict and making situations tougher on herself than necessary. She was taking home the toxicity of a bad meeting and losing sleep whenever an owner sent her a nasty email about something over which she had no control. She was coming across the same types of people and problems over and over again, "like dating the same boyfriend and needing to break that unhealthy pattern." So she started doing more "inner work" with a therapist, who helped her to see the connection between the career she chose and her childhood.

"When you spend your life trying to resolve other people's shit, it can be hard on a person," Ketty explains. "I didn't know where mine ended and others' started; I started putting more on the conflicts than I should have and internalized every little thing, however invalid. Even when a situation was preexisting and not of my making, I felt I was somehow part of the problem."

Her boundaries blurred to the point where she put enormous pressure on herself to resolve everyone else's issues quickly, and the emotional toll was starting to cloud her ability to see better solutions. She had the expertise to resolve most situations for her clients, "but I started getting defensive," Ketty recalls. "I fell into this thing where I wasn't seeing someone else's point of view because I'd believed I'd seen and knew it all. Maybe that was true, but I wasn't allowing new ideas or new perspectives to come to the table."

This epiphany transformed her approach to constructive conflict. While she continues to do her homework, she asks herself other important questions before she engages with rowdy condo owners, sidestepping contractors, or intractable zoning officials. If a project runs into problems, she asks herself at what point in time the issue turned into a conflict. She drills down to discover the underlying issue that was driving the conflict—a critical detail to understand, as oftentimes even the owners themselves don't know.

"Was it a contractor who was chosen? Was it my staff member? How am I a part of this? How am I *not* a part of this?"

Making it less personal while also understanding the backstory empowers Ketty to control the engagement when she gets in front of irate owners. She lets them speak first, allowing them to vent, then presents her list of options and solutions. When her adversaries storm into a meeting with false presumptions, providing clear information tends to quell most conflicts, but not always. When accusations are made that attack her personal integrity—"you're getting kickbacks" or "you don't care because you don't live here" or "you're helping so-and-so cook the books"—she calmly listens, then asks critical follow-up questions:

"So are you saying this?" or "What specifically are you accusing me of?" or "Can you please clarify where you got this information?"

Those questions are usually enough to mollify her accusers. If not, she goes back to her scrupulous record-keeping, including financial reports and every single email or communication she ever received on the matter, organized in a project management database. (Again, never hesitate to use technology as a conflict tool.) It's not that Ketty intends to throw the information back in their faces, but "people for whatever reason think they can deny the facts." Keeping an accurate and detailed history is one way to shut the conversation down before it drifts into destructive, time-wasting territory.

If the conflict still can't be resolved and she knows she's done everything she can to head off an escalation, she accepts there is nothing more she can do or say and simply asks the individual to send a demand letter to her attorney. But Ketty never lets it rise to the point of anger or resentment, at least on her part. When she enters these discussions, however volatile they can get, she understands that the owners she serves feel vulnerable. When conflicts come up, it's about their homes. Many are on fixed incomes and sensitive to the costs of maintenance and repairs. "And some are just off their rockers."

Today, she can chuckle at the absurdity of some of these confrontations, like the time some owners in a garden condo started sending her hate mail when her company locked up some hose bibs. They'd grown accustomed to using the outlets for their own gardening, but it was causing problems with the water supply, "yet you'd think we'd killed their first grandchildren!"

Ketty no longer dreads conflict. She recognizes that she can't make everyone happy. But doing all she can to put a problem to bed, knowing she did the right things for the right reasons, lessens the chance of a conflict coming to a head again. It also helps her to sleep at night.

Now Ketty sees these engagements as opportunities.

"People don't like conflict because they see it as confrontation, but I don't view it that way. Even though it can get a little messy sometimes, I see it as problem-solving."

Conflict at its best!

A Quick Scan

You don't necessarily have to go as deep as Ketty as you prepare for your encounter. But, whether it's a matter of reading people on the spot or stealthily gathering the information ahead of time, never walk into a situation unprepared. Even when something occurs at the last minute, there's no excuse not to do a quick scan of your adversary or a recon of conditions before you enter the engagement. A few smart questions and quick conversations with individuals close to the situation can reveal a lot, as can an online search if you know what to look for. Then, when circumstances permit, take a moment to clear your head and focus.

When I start filming a *Bar Rescue* episode, I purposely don't do advance research, because I don't want anything to contaminate my open-minded thoughts or cause me to decide who the heroes and villains will be. The most information I allow myself on the first day is a sixty-second briefing before I do the recon in my SUV. Once I am on set, I am data-driven, observing all the human dynamics and operational challenges with my own eyes.

By the next day my gears are turning. When my security people pick me up and drive me to the set, they're not allowed to talk or play the radio during the ride, which can take an hour or more depending on traffic. That's not because I'm being aloof. I am preparing myself. I am thinking of everything the people I am meeting with could say to me, and everything I could say back to them, the way chess masters plot out their match. I am thinking about their personalities, the problems they are facing, their environment, and any number of elements that might influence the way my ideas are received. So the interactions are not as spontaneous as they look on camera. Of course, I am never scripted. But, because of the level of preparation I do, it's extremely rare that I am going to walk into something that's a complete surprise to me.

I take the same approach to any business meeting. I typically leave my house twenty minutes earlier, giving myself forty minutes to an hour to completely clear my head of distractions and think through the coming interaction. If I know there's going to be a point of conflict with the person I am meeting with, you bet your ass I'll be ready for it. Even if the conflict isn't in that particular meeting, I've drawn a mental checklist of all the points I want to hit. Success won't come unless you are deliberate.

Doing your homework is necessary for any engagement that matters, whether or not it's a conflict. When I met my wife, Nicole, and decided that she was the one for me, I was intentional about what I wore, what I did, and what I said. I plotted out which restaurants I would take her to and which shows we would see. I paid attention to her likes and dislikes. Based on what I knew of her, I tried to imagine her preferences. Essentially, I was marketing myself to her. Make no mistake, our relationship is spontaneous, but it's the result of deliberate effort.

Winners prepare. Always. You can gain the advantage in a conflict before you even step into the ring. You can start out ahead of your adversary because most people don't think to put in all that work beforehand. By doing your homework, you will already be in the zone.

When you think about how a champion boxer prepares for a fight, you probably assume it's a combination of diet; roadwork; punching against hand pads, the heavy bag, the double-end bag; and sparring, and you'd be right. They polish their skills, strengthen their left and right hooks, and do all they can to get into peak physical condition. But they also prepare mentally. They study their opponents to first determine the type of fighter they're up against. Boxers don't step into the ring without studying how the other fighter ducks, weaves, and counterpunches. They condition themselves emotionally, with self-talk to build confidence and enhance focus. They develop an acute tactical awareness focused on pacing, countering their opponents, with goals and game plans they can switch up within seconds, depending on the direction the fight is taking.

Actor Jimmy Smits, who played boxer Arturo Ortega in *Price of Glory*, studied the psychology of the sport as he prepared for this role, and came up with one of the most insightful comments that perfectly sums up the fundamentals of engagement, and how best to prepare for any kind of conflict:

"It's less about the physical training, in the end, than it is about the mental preparation: boxing is a chess game: You have to be skilled enough and have trained hard enough to know how many different ways you can counterattack in any situation, at any moment."

Undefeated World Boxing Organization female flyweight Nicola Adams also likens this blood sport to chess, where you "encourage your opponent to make mistakes so you can capitalize on it. People think you get in the ring and see the red mist, but it's not about aggression. Avoiding getting knocked out is tactical."

For all the flying fists and knockouts, you can dominate in the ring through mental agility or, as Floyd Mayweather puts it, "He can have heart, he can hit harder and he can be stronger, but there's no fighter smarter than me."

Constructive conflict, whatever form it takes, is a combination of passion, energy, courage, and conviction, but you won't land that winning punch without the mental agility that comes from really knowing your subject. I can think of few professional sports that do not involve intensive pregame study. Tennis players and their coaches train by watching footage of past matches involving themselves and/or their future opponents. They use ball-tracking artificial intelligence to predict their opponent's next move.

Think about all the other technology that now exists in professional sports. Athletes wear "smart clothing" with sensors woven in to detect and relay real-time data to their coaches or trainers, with three-dimensional motion-capture technology that times and pinpoints motion. This wearable technology can measure anything in real time, including heart rate, temperature, hydration, and exertion. The live metrics tell them when to rest, stretch, or train harder. Performance-, data-, and video-analysis software also improves decision-making not just based on a football, basketball, baseball, or hockey player's own individual performance, but the strengths and vulnerabilities of members of the opposing team. It's taking doing your homework before a competitive engagement to a whole new level.

Even without the advantage of these cutting-edge, hairsplitting preparation tools, there is nothing stopping the rest of us from stepping into our own arenas armed with precise knowledge and helpful, detailed analysis of our opponents. Think about successful lawyers and prosecutors who do their version of predictive analytics their own way. They don't rely on hearsay and assumptions; they gather data and evidence and road test it. They cross-examine their own clients and witnesses before they even think about entering a courtroom, to expose any weaknesses and address them. If you really care about the outcome of your engagement, you'd be wise to do the same.

Order in the Court

When you are well prepared, you don't have to be aggressive to dominate in a conflict situation. Miami attorney Richard John "Johnny" Bartz is not exactly the confrontational type. Outside the courtroom or mediation conference table, he is soft-spoken, deferential, and diplomatic. In fact, he *hates* conflict—at least in the destructive sense of the term. But he has a consistent track record for positive results in his divorce cases because of the way he prepares. He's a formidable adversary because he spends hours studying case precedents and assembling the evidence that gives him the confidence to calmly argue in favor of his clients, no matter how complex or contentious the cases may be.

"Good lawyering is all about your game plan and approach to confidential information that the other side doesn't know," Johnny explains. "If you go through what those outcomes might be, then you will be much better prepared and more likely to get the best result."

Johnny spends a lot of time putting himself inside the minds of the presiding judge, imagining what that person might say given the evidence, and constantly updating himself on decisions made in similar or higher courts in Florida. He also makes his clients the subject of intensive study, knowing from past experience that what they *say* they want may not be what they *actually* want. And he tries to understand the mindset of the opposing party to get ahead of what their attorney's arguments are likely to be. He explores multiple scenarios, trying to make legal arguments and find evidence that refutes whatever the other side's narrative might be.

That level of preparation can take eighty hours or more, although Johnny doesn't necessarily bill clients for all that research. That deep dive he makes in the discovery process is part of the fun. It's "like putting together the pieces of a jigsaw puzzle" as he wades through bank statements, credit cards, and lists of assets, uncovering as much as he can for clients whose properties and investments are often spread across the globe or well hidden inside complex corporate structures. But, as he figures out what a fair division of marital assets might look like, he's also weighing what is more important to each party, because it can be beneficial to give the other side a win and make them feel better about a final settlement.

"Everyone has something they value more than other aspects of their property, and you have to get to the bottom of what that is. It's my job to probe a little and recognize what is based on pure emotion and what is coming from a rational frame of mind. Then I bring them down to earth, explaining the options and ramifications, all the while accepting that it is ultimately my client's decision."

For Johnny's practice, the end goal is a speedy, equitable solution more than winning itself.

"A lot of lawyers have this drive to fight and get one over, but when you engage in that type of behavior, so does your opposing counsel, and you end up in this negative feedback loop. Of course, when someone is being unreasonable, I'll build a case and throw the book at them. But all those sassy recantations of law and case precedents that prove the other side is wrong don't have much benefit when they get you further away from a settlement."

Johnny has built his reputation as someone who is willing to meet halfway in a mediation conference, though he will not cave to the other party's excessive demands. A nasty *War of the Roses* divorce, when the case gets snarled in court for months or even years, is the very opposite of constructive conflict. That kind of divorce may bring in plenty of revenue through billable hours, but Johnny prefers the quick and clean resolution that can come from a thoroughly researched case.

"The angrier and more adversarial it gets, the sloppier the outcome and the greater the chance of really ruining relationships," he explains.

While he avoids taking on the cases that are about gouging exes for the most money and hurting each other, any of these conflicts can spiral. The result of a drawn-out divorce is an estranged couple who can never look each other in the eye and can't even agree on where and when to pick up the kids for their time on the shared custody schedule. It's the children who suffer most.

Knowing these stakes gives Johnny a knot in the pit of his stomach each time he goes before a judge. There are also professional and reputational consequences to the kind of lawyering that's ill prepared, aggressive, or emotional. Presiding judges are impartial, but pushing for certain things too hard or showing an unwillingness to concede on any points will ultimately tip the scales against a client. His relationships with members of the legal system and other practitioners are also a long game that can impact his brand and have a ripple effect on present and future cases. That's why Johnny pulls back for a few beats when exchanges become too intense.

"Being in adversarial mode is fast-paced and can quickly get out of hand, which is scary because all you say is on the record," Johnny explains. "You never want to say something that will compromise you or your client, so say nothing at all as you think and formulate your strategy. Maintaining a cool head in combination with the facts helps you think out your response. But once you are in the adrenaline zone, you can lose your critical-thinking abilities."

Johnny gets especially nervous the day and night before hearings, which tend to be hectic, with tight timelines and piles of data from forensic audits that he does his best to commit to memory. But, again, good preparation always pays off in the moment, when everything seems to slow down and the answers in his thick case binder come to him as if by magic.

What keeps Johnny's head clear as he enters the ring are the best interests of his clients, often the underdogs in the most complex cases. He is especially passionate about protecting birthrights and parental rights, which can include a nonbiological stay-at-home mother in a gay marriage whose financial support and access as a mom is under threat. Or a biological father whose long work hours forced him to miss a couple of prenatal visits, unfairly painting him in a bad light and risking all future access to his child. Johnny has also been venturing into immigration law, ensuring that a young gay man doesn't get deported back to the home country he fled after being jailed and tortured for who he was.

"That's where the law is powerful," says Johnny. "That's where all the homework finally pays off: allowing someone to be a part of the life of their child or to stay in the country they struggled so hard to make their home."

It's the kind of win that can only happen when you do the work.

Taffer Toolkit Takeaways

1. *Assume nothing.* Before you begin a discussion that may escalate into something more serious, know what you know—and what you don't know—about the situation.

2. *Focus your research.* Imagine what information you would use if you were on the other side of the debate, then gather enough evidence to shoot those points down!

3. *Steer it back to what you know.* If you don't know where a set of statistics or "facts" were sourced or if they are even true, don't allow yourself to be distracted.

4. *Think deeply about the source of the conflict.* Ask yourself important questions to understand the root cause, the timeline of the issue, and what role, if any, you played in escalating the conflict. Be self-aware.

5. *Let them speak first, allowing them to vent.* This can help cool down the temperature, yield more information, and allow yourself more time to think of an answer or solution.

6. *Know the backstory.* Keeping an accurate and detailed history is one way to shut the conversation down before it drifts into destructive, time-wasting territory.

7. ***Do a quick recon.*** A few smart questions and quick conversations with individuals close to the situation can reveal a lot, as can an online search if you know what to look for. Then, when circumstances permit, take a moment to clear your head and focus.

8. ***Get an early start.*** If you head out a half hour or so early to the site of the engagement, it will give you more time to think through the coming interaction. Keep a checklist in the back of your head of all the points you want to hit.

6

TO YELL OR NOT TO YELL

Calculate when to go there. Leverage your passion with strategy.

Jack's Fire Department, a bar in Queens, New York, owned and operated by three Irish brothers who were also members of the FDNY, was going down in flames. Brian, Jimmy, and John Mc-Gowan had inherited the bar from their father, but they couldn't stop fighting over how to run the business, and they were making a bunch of rookie mistakes. I had to knock their heads together, but at least one of them, Jimmy, wasn't taking too kindly to my suggestions.

Jimmy was a boozer with a fondness for brawling. Really, he was the source of many of the problems because his violent temper was out of control, and you cannot bring that kind of energy into a place of business, or in life, for that matter. When I did my usual test run of the bar, filling it with a thirsty crowd to properly diagnose the operational challenges, it wasn't going well, and Jimmy started acting out with the cameras rolling. He was being nasty to his wife and female staff, and disrespectful to his siblings. I'd had enough.

The only way to reach hotheads like that is to get loud. I charged in like a bull. Jimmy was a big, muscular guy. I knew he could take me if he wanted to, but not when I was already right on him like that. I was inches from his face; we were spitting all over each other as we screamed. I could tell he was getting ready to hit me, but I had the advantage because I knew how things would play out. His pupils were large, like those of a cat getting ready to pounce, so I moved in closer, grabbed his wrists, gave them a couple of love squeezes, and watched his pupils go down. He stepped away from me and started pacing.

"You couldn't pull it off, so you curse at your wife, and you drink!" I told him, then landed the final blow. "You're failing because you're an asshole!"

Then I told his brothers, "Either he is leaving this bar now, or I am."

They duly kicked him out, but Jimmy wasn't done. He came back in through the rear door, went behind the bar, and spat a mouthful of whiskey in the face of his older sibling (they were all well past forty), then walked out again. With the night thus turned sour, Brian and John ushered out their customers and closed up the bar. The next day, his brothers and I sat Jimmy down and set him straight. The previous intense confrontation broke him wide open, and, in the sober light of day, he was more prepared to listen.

There is a time and a place for escalating the conflict. There's a flow to the discussion and, as it intensifies, you have a choice: to go there and raise it to the level of yelling, or to step out. In a positive, constructive conflict, either one of those decisions may be appropriate. But it must be your decision. You, and you alone, can size up the situation and decide whether to use your passion to land a point, and how far to take it.

Some techniques for powering your voice and body language in conflict include:

- **Watching the dilation of eyes.** As the pupils get smaller, your adversary is being less emotional and reactionary. It's in that moment of calm you are more likely to be heard.

- **Checking the rest of the body language.** If they are standing with their arms folded, for example, they're tensed up and shutting down. Facial signs of rising anger include a clenched jaw, furrowed brow, and a flushing of the skin and intensely focused eye contact.

- **Reengaging.** It's at that moment, when my adversary is trying to put up an emotional wall, that I bring my voice down, lean in, and get them to drop their arms with a touch on the hand or the shoulder to release the tension. Then I go in for another hit. Think of it as a sparring match.

Again, this is about using your emotions strategically. Think about the ways we build toward getting good and mad. Our language is full of expressions that we use without really taking the time to think them through—handy sayings that convey a lot of meaning. And so it is with how we talk about anger. When we describe what it's like to get really pissed off, we often use an image of impaired vision: "I was so mad, I saw red." "I was in a blind fury." "He made me so mad, I couldn't see straight." These metaphors convey a profound truth that you should take to heart when preparing for conflict. It won't matter one bit that you have done your homework or made your cost-benefit calculation if you let your emotions rule over your head. Conflict driven by pure emotion is doomed to failure.

Master of Emotions

I'll let you in on a secret. When I'm taping my shows, smashing poorly made cocktails and plates of inedible food onto the floor, listing at the top of my voice all that's wrong with a bar—I am not actually in a state of rage. In fact, once the scene has been shot, as I walk out of the bar and past my production team, it's customary for me to turn to them and wink. The passion is real. In that moment I am being sincere, because I care about the small businesses I am trying to rescue. But I choose exactly when to crank up the volume. I am in full control, and yelling is part of an overall strategy.

It's a rare occurrence, but whenever I was not the master of my emotions, when it was *true* rage, I paid a price.

It happens. We're human. Looking back on those rare instances, I can't say I'd have done anything differently, because I am hardwired to protect those I love. But when things become too personal, too emotional, the engagement can make a situation worse than when it started. So if at all possible, avoid putting yourself in that position in the first place.

Passion versus Anger

When passion gets overtaken by anger, your adversaries will revel in your rage, because they can see they've gotten under your skin. Like a lawyer cross-examining a hostile witness, they will begin to manipulate to win, intentionally provoking you further. They realize that your emotions have caused you to loosen your grip on the logical thread of the overall argument and you are no longer thinking clearly. But you already know this. You already force yourself to calm down before tackling an issue that could escalate into conflict. As well you should. Still, that doesn't mean emotions—even strong ones—don't have an important role to play when you engage in conflict. They do.

There is a fine line between passion and anger. Anger does not serve positive conflict well because it reduces communication and causes greater resistance, prompting the opponent to dig in. *Angry* emotion is the enemy of positive conflict. You end up with confusion, not resolution. On the other hand, passionate emotion is conviction and causes engagement.

To understand the difference, imagine there is a meter inside the brain that measures what happens when emotion meets engagement with the colors green and red. When the meter starts lighting up in the red zone, it means that the person on the other side of the engagement is no longer listening to you, much less agreeing. It means you have completely lost them. If you don't want that person to shut down, you need to lower your tone or say something positive to bring them back into the green zone. I call this my "conflict dashboard," which allows me to move in and out of each zone according to whatever it is I am trying to accomplish from the conflict, keeping everyone engaged.

I learned early on in life how to manage the reactions of others. My mother had an undiagnosed disorder that resulted in her having a hair-trigger temper. I grew up in an era when psychiatric problems weren't discussed and people rarely sought treatment because of the stigma surrounding mental health issues, Mom included. But my best guess is that she suffered from some form of manic depression. Her anger ventured into the psychotic, and the slightest thing could send her into a physically abusive rage. She was tall and strikingly beautiful—an imposing figure who worked full-time as a runway model. And she had an outsized personality to match those looks—like a redheaded firecracker who could explode at any time, but with a much bigger bang. In public, it was embarrassing. In private, it was terrifying.

When I was thirteen, my mother became so incensed about something I said or did that she picked up my drum set and hit me with it so hard, she broke my arm. That was an important lesson for me. I blamed the incident on myself because I knew better how to handle her. All it would take was a messy bedroom, a bad school grade, an object broken in the house, or something even less significant to set her off and cause me bodily harm. So I already understood that how she reacted to me in any given moment was critical to how the rest of my day would go. I'd been fielding my mother's rage ever since I could crawl. I'd also witnessed destructive conflict between my mother and stepfather, whose arguments routinely got loud and physically violent. But in the case of the drums, I failed to use the skills I'd already instinctively developed, and the situation got out of hand.

As a child, I took control of my circumstances by watching my mother closely. I became highly sensitive to her reactions and how she received what someone, me especially, was saying. By the age of eight, I had the receptors to read her mood based on facial expressions, tone, physical disposition. . . . I had to watch out for those cues for the sake of my own well-being. I could move her from a place of frustration or disappointment to happiness or laughter with a well-timed joke or goofy expression.

Manipulating her mood by my actions had a huge impact on my own happiness. I played cute. Family members would come over and expect me to be the ham. Because Mom was amused, she was less inclined to smack me. Eventually, I learned how to push all her buttons to my advantage. I could steer the conversation in a different direction by nodding as I was speaking, subliminally getting her to agree with me. I could tell if her arms were crossed whether she was receiving it, then process the data and adjust accordingly.

I became a master of the art of deflection. If we were all at the dinner table and my mother started questioning me about skipping Hebrew school, for example, I would sit up in my chair and say something to my sister to create a different conversation. Instead of slumping with a deer-in-the-headlights expression, I kept my disposition bright and innocent. I used my actions, words to pull her out of that dark hole of rage she was about to dive into, rather than let her pull me in with her. And I would change the topic in a way that would stick for at least a minute or two—just long enough for the dark cloud to pass. It got to the point where I wasn't even conscious that I was controlling her reactions in this way. The way other people can take a breath without thinking about it, I could switch it up mid-sentence and change what I said, self-correcting or self-editing on a dime.

Looking back, I guess it's no surprise I minored in social anthropology in college. I studied primates and how these animals behaved within their own societies. I learned that there are certain primal instincts we all have. Our animal instincts cause us to land somewhere emotionally, and when you pay attention, when you are aware of that place someone is in, you can adjust that initial emotion.

All these experiences became my inspiration for reaction management, a concept I explored in my first book, *Raise the Bar: An Action-Based Method for Maximum Customer Reactions*.[1] In a nutshell, reaction management is about engineering emotions. By knowing what to look for and closely monitoring body language, you can tell exactly what words to say or actions to take to elicit the response you want from an individual. This translates to both personal conflict situations as well as business. Whatever you are selling—music, food, or beverage; any type of consumer product or service; or simply your point of view on an issue—whoever creates the best reactions wins. And if something doesn't create a reaction, it's meaningless.

What was at first unconscious became entirely intentional. I said to myself, "Okay, everything I do has to create a reaction. That's how I get noticed in a crowd. That's how I get people to read what I need them to read. That's how I get attention. That's how I get responses. I have to create reactions."

I became confident in my ability to feel what others are feeling in the moment, whether they are angry or happy, frustrated or fearful. I can play in the arena of my adversaries' feelings, because they are not unknowns to me. I can push them to a point of frustration and bring them back out of it, always knowing where the line is as I watch for the pupils to dilate, or muscles tightening in the neck. Knowing just when to yell, how loud to get, and when to stop truly is an art. Or, more accurately, a delicate dance, except that those on the other side of the conflict have no idea how they are being led.

Years later, when I ran the Troubadour nightclub during the height of the punk rock era, this skill came in handy. Artists and bands like Black Flag, Adam Ant, Sid Vicious, and Fear would draw crowds that bounced around the dance floor on pogo sticks and swung heavy metal chains. These guys are probably executives now, but at the time it wasn't considered a great night out unless someone got bruised or cut. Punk audiences were notorious for rushing the stage and violently crashing into each other—what was known as slam dancing. So I had to muster all my reaction management experience to deal with these unruly music fans. When I had to deal with a jerk or throw out a drunk, if I didn't come in full tilt, yelling and causing them to question their own aggressiveness, I would lose. Knowing exactly when to come in hard, then modulate to a softer tone has been my saving grace. Not once have I been hit throughout my entire career in the bar, restaurant, and music industries.

Within the yelling, there are also subtle gradations of volume and tone. Watch me on *Bar Rescue* enough times and you'll notice my method. I'm engaged in constant self-talk as I monitor the reactions of bar owners and staff. Despite the twists and turns, I am purposeful, and I know exactly where I am going. I may not know exactly how I am going to get there, but I am moving through a process, making deductive points and affirmations, pushing the owners as far as they can go before pulling them back in. You'll see me using nonverbal cues, like holding my hand up flat to say *Stop!* or reaching in for a hug before verbally punching them. It's a constant push-me pull-me of affirmations and challenges to break them down. I'm tilling the soil until they are ready to receive some seeds of wisdom, and the process isn't pretty. My volume plays a critical role from beginning to end, but context and purpose are critical not just to when I yell, but *how* I yell.

Gutterball!

Take, for example, the Lucky 66 bowling alley and bar I rescued in the Season Seven episode "Gutterball!" Put plainly, owner Mike Draper was an asshole. Turnover was so high, he couldn't keep bar staff for more than a couple of months. Mike had installed a gym upstairs to work out and blow off steam so he wouldn't scream at people, but it wasn't working. He'd fired Miles, his bowling alley technician, nine times! Mike was obnoxious not just to his staff, including his son Jay and his granddaughter Daphne, but the customers! He owed $1 million on the place and was losing another $10,000 to $15,000 a month as more and more customers voted with their feet.

While Lucky 66 was popular enough in the years after Mike bought it in 2003, in its previous five years of business, profits started drying up as bowling alleys became less of a destination. He hadn't done much to enhance its curb appeal, with a small sign on a nondescript building with peeling white paint in a strip mall off Route 66 near Albuquerque, New Mexico. Physically and operationally, there was a lot of runway for improvement. But the real problem was Mike's attitude.

"I don't share the philosophy that the customer is always right," he informed my producers.

I'd sent over three young people to do recon for me. First, he ignored their requests for water.

"I'll be with you when I'm done, okay?" he told them. "If you are trying to get under my skin, you are getting there. . . ."

Then, after two rounds of shots, he tried to cut them off, asking one of the young men how much he weighed. Mike was not only rude, disrespecting the biggest spenders in the room, he was physically threatening as he put his hand on the guy's shoulder and said:

"I'm not serving you anymore. You got a bit smart to the wrong person. I am the owner, and you will leave!"

It was time to *really* get under Mike's skin, so I came in with all guns blazing. I was incredulous that a bar owner who was bleeding cash would have the audacity to treat new customers this way. So I yelled with an appropriate blend of anger and disgust in my tone as I challenged him on the behavior I'd just witnessed.

"Do they appear intoxicated to you?" I asked Mike, not bothering to wait for the answer. "How would you feel if I put my hand on your shoulder like you did to him and pretty much said, 'I don't like you and I want you to leave here because I said so'?"

"I guess I'd be upset," Mike mumbled.

"Because the person who did that to you would be an ass!" I shouted. "Why were you an ass to him, Mike?"

"I'm sorry, I don't have an answer for you," he said.

Then I called in the whole team: Jay; Joel and Joel Jr., the father-son duo who owned the food concession; and Miles and his son, who kept the thirty-six bowling lanes functioning. Really, this was a family business comprised of three families. They should have been fully supportive of each other. But Mike's behavior wasn't allowing that to happen. He was pushing everyone away.

"Jay, simple question. Does your father act like an ass, or *is* he an ass?"

"He's an asshole," Jay said, still angry about the way his father had treated his daughter a month earlier, accusing her of not working hard enough, among other things.

"How does that feel, Mike? How much are you in debt, Mike?" I asked, injecting some real venom into my voice.

"A lot."

"Do you like writing a check for fifteen thousand dollars every month?"

"I don't."

"When you do that, do you say to yourself, 'I'm an asshole'?"

"No, I have not."

"Maybe it's time to say that to yourself, Mike!"

I was on a roll. I was rubbing Mike's face in his own mess. I was on a mission to humiliate him and make him feel the way he made others feel who'd been on the other end of his abrasiveness. I took an informal poll of the rest of his team:

"Is Mike an ass?" I asked them, one by one. "Yes," they all told me, "he is!"

"Not one person in this room believes you have the ability to not be an ass!" I screamed at Mike. "I am not sure I want to help you to get it back. Why would I make this beautiful so that you can perpetuate your ass-ness? If I built the Taj Mahal, your ass-ness would destroy it!"

At this point Mike had been thoroughly chastened. As I was yelling, I was observing how Mike was receiving what I had to say. At first, he could barely hold his head up to look me in the eye. But the more I threw those loud verbal punches, the straighter he stood, facing me and taking it, like he knew it was for his own good. The engagement meter was still very much in the green zone. It was as if he were back in the army, taking orders. *Sir, yes, sir!* I could almost hear inside his brain. This was interesting, so I pushed him further.

"Are you disrespectful to people?" I asked him.

"I am disrespectful."

"So an ass who is disrespectful to people. Does that type of person deserve to make money?"

"No."

"There is a god after all!" I exclaimed, then turned to face the rest of the room. "Mike got exactly what he deserved, didn't he? A million dollars in debt and a family who doesn't even believe in him!"

On that note I walked out the door, letting him know I wasn't even sure if I wanted to put in the work for a guy like him.

"I can play tougher than you!" I told him as I turned my back on him. "Good night, Mike! Clean your freakin' bar, asshole!"

My whole purpose in behaving that way toward Mike, besides giving him a taste of his own medicine, was to get his attention and respect. Yes, calling someone an asshole in front of his whole family and staff was personal. But I was attacking his behavior—the way he was treating others—not the man. I knew there had to be more to him than what I was seeing on the surveillance camera. Mike was a Vietnam veteran. He'd walked through fire and seen things the people in his orbit couldn't imagine. I needed to communicate with him in a way that he could not just dismiss. As he said later, "Nobody's yelled at me like that since I was in the army. I was put in my place!"

It was exactly what Mike needed in that moment to wake up and see what he was doing to himself, his family, and his business. His bowling alley maintenance man, Miles, and his family had $400 in the bank and would be kicked out of their home on the first of the month if Lucky 66 were to close down. Daphne, Mike's granddaughter, who'd dreamed of owning and running the place from the time she was just seven years old, would lose her inheritance. Mike, who opened the bowling alley to honor his late father, a bowling champion, would lose all he'd worked so hard for. His life savings would go down the toilet. Worse, he was on the brink of alienating the people he loved most in the world. But instead of stepping up and accepting responsibility for his failure, he blamed everyone around him. He pushed the very people away who could help him fix the problem, especially Daphne, who had proved extremely capable at running all aspects of the operations, from the bar to the bowling machinery.

I needed to get to the bottom of why Mike was sabotaging himself. Before things started to go wrong, Mike had been a force for good in the community. But money troubles can be debilitating. When you live in constant fear of losing it all, you internalize the insecurity and sense of failure. Mike's response was to become a hard-ass. No one, not even Daphne, could measure up. I guess it was much easier than shining the light on himself. So I did it for him. I knew that if he couldn't change his attitude, he wouldn't be able to change his future, so I dished it back at him to jolt him awake.

The next day, Mike was the model of humility. My method worked because he'd finally encountered someone who could call him on his BS. He responded to me because I acted like his drill sergeant, and deep down he knew I was bawling him out for his own good. As someone coming in from the outside, I could confront Mike more easily with that level of strength than the people closest to him, and it was exactly what he needed. I have so much respect for people who served in the military, and I understood that having fought in a war, Mike was probably dealing with some trauma that made him respond to stressful situations differently than most. He didn't know how to reach out and ask for help. But the result was that he'd become so negative, bitter, and unlikeable that no one was rooting for him.

Mike was beginning to grasp this fact, so I turned down the volume. But I *still* wasn't done. I brought in Daphne, his estranged granddaughter, to join Jay and the rest of the team, and gently made him face her. It was already clear to me that this young lady had his heart, and that being at odds with her had just about broken him.

"This is your granddaughter. Good or bad, she's been trying. What do you have to say to her?"

"Sorry . . ."

"What else? You can't do this alone. . . . Do you get that? The two people best equipped to help you are your son and granddaughter. Tell them!"

"I need you to help me go forward," Mike told them. Then, to his granddaughter: "I need you. Since you left, why do I want to put the effort into it?"

Mike finally admitted there was no point in owning a successful business if those he loved weren't a part of it. He choked up as he spoke. We all did. I was proud of him because it wasn't an easy thing for an old warrior like him to admit.

"I haven't told people I wanted them since Vietnam," Mike said.

The rest of the rescue was easy. Mike kept doling out the bear hugs. Within twenty-four hours Mike had become Mr. Hospitality. He was all smiles as he greeted his customers, and he kept up the positive attitude even as things went wrong, as they always do, during my stress test. The face-lift we gave to the bar, the training we gave to the staff, and the necessary technology upgrades put the establishment which we called the Great 66 Entertainment Center, on a path to success. But the most important feature of this rescue was the upgrade to Mike's outlook and behavior toward others. He'd rediscovered a graciousness that drew people in and kept them coming back.

Few things matter more to me than family and the people who serve, and this business combined both. I was so moved by Mike and his spectacular turnaround that, at the end of the episode, I handed him a $10,000 check out of my own pocket to help him cover expenses before revenues started rolling back in. Mike wasn't really an asshole. He was just a man in pain, and my trademark yelling at full blast was the cure.

Breaking Brandon

There's never a show where I don't yell. There's always that moment when I need to shock an owner into changing an unhealthy pattern. The employees can't and, in most cases, the loved ones won't, say what they need to hear at a volume level that will penetrate. But I don't always go for the jugular the way I did with Mike. If I'd done that to Brandon Purser, owner of Linda Lou's Time for Two in Layton, Utah, he'd have shut down on me completely and his bar would have closed for good.

It had been Brandon's dream to own a bar ever since he did a school paper on the industry at the age of twelve. Linda Lou's, a local dive bar in a strip mall, presented that opportunity when it came up for sale six years prior. But he had it all going against him. The place was a dump. He had zero experience. Under Utah state law, a bar also had to sell food, so they kept their personal deep fryer at the bar to cook soggy chicken wings, which stunk up the place. Everything was broken, including the sump pump, which constantly flooded behind the bar, and they never replenished, so more than half the items on the cocktail menu could not be made. The result was dwindling customers and losses of up to $8,000. The joint was just four days from closing. Meanwhile, Brandon's mother, Winona, who I was told suffered from MS, struggled to run the place during the daytime and sank the last few thousand of her retirement savings to keep it afloat.

Brandon felt so guilty about his failure that he completely checked out. His three loyal bartenders, like family to him, were desperate for his support, but he hid in the back office doing God knows what on his computer. We did recon from the empty unit next door and watched his well-meaning, untrained staff botch the most basic cocktails to the point where I couldn't watch anymore. I stormed in and made a scene, tossing drinks and dumping greasy chicken all over the bar.

"This bar is such a shithole, I can be spilling stuff all night and it really doesn't freaking matter, does it?" I growled. "Guys, is there one reason why you would come in this bar? Food, drinks, environment? Is there any reason to come into this bar?"

Silence and headshakes all around.

"And, Brandon, where have you been all night?"

"In my office."

"Is it time-sensitive?"

"No."

"'So screw all of you, I am going to go in the back and sit at my computer.' Gee, I wonder why he's failing? Why are you failing, Brandon? Do you care?"

"I do but I don't," he answered.

"Do you care about your mother's money? Do you care about her?"

"Yeah."

"What the fuck?! What the fuck?! Why do you take your mother's money and not show up, Brandon? Why do you go hide in the back, Brandon? Why did you do this in the first place, Brandon, to leave your mother here?"

Silence.

"Give me an answer, Brandon, please! Give me a friggin' answer, *why*?"

I wasn't trying to squish the man. I was trying to wake him up and see if he had the slightest interest in saving his bar. I had to knock the apathy out of the guy. I thought it was lousy that he hadn't even told his employees that they might be out of a job in four days, no pay, no notice. They loved him and felt for him, and that was their reward? And I couldn't do the rescue if he'd already given up. This was probably the most dysfunctional bar I'd seen in seven seasons of doing the show, so fixing it in four days was going to be a challenge and I wasn't about to waste my time on a man who stayed slumped in his office hiding from the mess he'd created.

As I left, I ordered his staff to go home and leave Brandon to clean up the bar. Once more, I yelled.

"Brandon will do it! Brandon will clear the bar tonight! Brandon will be accountable! Brandon will be successful at something tonight! At least this little area will be clean!"

It wasn't sustained screaming. Unlike with Mike, I kept the loud part of the interaction brief because I knew he could only take so much. Watching Brandon's reaction to my scolding, I could tell I was close to the line. His engagement meter wasn't in the red zone yet, but it sure was lighting up yellow. I took it as far as I could. He needed to hear his name. He was in some kind of dissociative mental state, and I wanted to snap him back into reality and confront the situation. The people around him were giving him a pass and it wasn't doing him any favors. Sometimes, to stop someone walking off a cliff, you must grab him roughly by the neck and yank him back onto solid ground.

The next day, I decided not to raise my voice. I calmly laid out the facts and everything that was at stake. I itemized the problems and got halfway through the checklist when Brandon broke down in tears and went into the men's room. The previous night's confrontation had shaken him to his core and when he got home, he couldn't sleep. By the next morning he was in complete meltdown mode and couldn't manage anything I had to throw at him. The poor guy was torn between taking care of his failing business and taking care of his parents with failing health. If he was home, he felt guilty he wasn't managing the business, and if he was at the bar, he felt guilty he wasn't looking after his family. The poor guy felt like he couldn't win.

I knew that if I didn't help him deal with the pressure, I couldn't help the bar, so I sent him home.

"Right now you don't have the strength you need to do this, and I get it," I told him. "Go home, take a nap, and when you come back tonight, sit there like an owner and watch them come through for you."

The rest of the show was about getting creative with the cocktail menu, turning the place into a fun speakeasy that would become a neighborhood destination, and training up the staff to become skilled mixologists. They were bubbly and bright people. I'd sit at the bar with them every day. Those personalities, combined with a great and executable drinks list, would make Linda Lou's a success. Now everyone had a purpose: to fight for Brandon's smile.

In every *Bar Rescue* episode, I'm fighting for the owner's and/or employees, lives and businesses, not mine. When I yell, and how I yell, is strategic. The more you listen, the more you will notice that there are subtle variations depending on the circumstances and the person on the other side of the confrontation. Again, I may *look* angry, but I am not angry at them. . . . They did not hurt me! At the end of a day's filming, I get to go home to my successful business, wonderful family, and happy life. I *am*, though, passionate about helping these folks. Communicating effectively while maintaining an emotionally engaged, not angry persona is the most critical and difficult element to successful conflict. The moment emotions become angry, meaningful conflict becomes conflict without purpose, even blind rage. Conflict based upon anger always comes with a high price and little chance for a meaningful result.

The other side of the emotional coin—the one you will never find me on—is eliminating all emotion when you engage in conflict. But you are a person, not a robot, and understanding your emotions, and using them to communicate passionately, is key to positive conflict.

Taffer Toolkit Takeaways

1. *Be the master of your emotions.* Yelling should never be the product of actual rage. Do it for effect, all the while checking for the physiological reactions of your adversary so they neither explode nor shut down.

2. *Understand the difference between passion and anger.* Yes, there should be sincere emotion behind the yelling. But, when passion gets overtaken by anger, your adversaries will revel in your rage, because they can see they've gotten under your skin. Always be in control of the exchange, no matter how emotional it gets.

3. *Manage the reactions of others.* This is all about getting your message across with impact. Control the volume and tone of your voice according to how your points are landing. Manipulate through the power of voice.

4. *Mix up the recipe.* Yelling should be combined with more subtle tricks that you can apply using your voice and physical presence when you are in a verbal altercation, from connection tools like eye contact, to physical proximity.

5. *Know when to switch it off.* There is nothing to be gained by continuing to yell after you've made your point. Once the engagement is over, you are done!

7

LISTEN TO WIN

Purposeful conflict is not just about being heard.
Your adversary's words matter too.

In the early days of filming my show, when I was a rookie to the world of television, the producers made me put an earwig, or wireless receiver, inside my ear. Almost all reality show personalities wear these devices because producers typically tell them what to say. Many judges on the Food Network, for example, are fed what to say and do. They're told to take one step over to the left of the camera or are reminded of the name of a contestant they are about to speak to. Frankly, the earpiece has come in handy when I'm being filmed and there are eight employees in the line in front of me. I'm good with faces; names, not so much.

Of course, it's my own words and actions that are driving the scene. On *Bar Rescue*, nothing has been scripted because I wanted my show to be authentic from the outset. But something happens when a producer goes on for more than a couple of sentences. I can't figure out who to listen to: myself or the person on the other side of the camera who is giving direction right inside my ear canal. My head is no longer in the present moment.

It's similar to when you're having an intense discussion with someone. Your heart is beating fast and the adrenaline is pumping. All you're really thinking about is the next thing you're going to say, and your lips can't wait to start moving. But, while all this is happening, you're not really hearing them. Instead, you are constructing that next argument in your head and missing some critical information. And, on the other side, they're not really hearing *you*. Nothing is being gained by the interaction.

This is why it pays to slow it down. Force yourself to listen. And don't be scared of the silence, because, in constructive conflict, silence can be your friend. It helps both sides digest the information. Whenever there is a long pause in a debate, you'll notice that the first person to jump in usually loses the point. It makes them uncomfortable, so they rush to fill the void with a weak statement or argument. Meanwhile, those who are okay in those pockets of silence are already several moves ahead, watching, waiting, and gathering the information that will help them slam-dunk their argument. Let that long, awkward pause work in your favor!

Let Them Finish

Other cues to watch for and leverage during conflict include:

- **Your opponent's stance.** Notice the arms. Are they crossed and folded? Is there a tightness around the mouth and eyes, are the eyebrows lowered and fists clenched? Is the face flushed? Do something fast, a word or gesture, to ease the tension before they shut down completely.

- **Vocal patterns.** Is the pitch rising? Is the tone harsh? Do you hear a torrent of words? Stand your ground, relax your own facial expression and stance, and hold your ground and maintain silence. Let them finish, and resist the temptation to mirror your opponent's aggressive behavior. Instead, use the levels of emotion, yours and theirs, in the service of the moment.

- **Authentic emotion.** As they start revealing their true feelings, utilize the words "Really?" or "Wow! And?" These are inviting terms of engagement that make your opponent feel good and tell you how he or she really feels. They are among the greatest tools for conflict because, when properly used, you'll get to the primal reason why someone is acting a certain way.

Sometimes on *Bar Rescue* I can be so intimidating that people shut down on me. Conflict *must* be engaging. That's why it's crucial to leverage your listening skills and remain hyper-aware of your opponent's emotional reactions using the conflict dashboard I described in the previous chapter. Full engagement with your opponent requires more than listening. It is about bringing all the physical, emotional, and verbal cues into your awareness.

There are multiple ways to understand people, beyond the words they speak, and when you pay attention to these cues, you can control the flow of the discussion, even to the point of managing your opposition's emotions or, again, reaction management. Again, it's helpful to shake your head or nod in the direction that you want their views to go, for example. Subliminally, those are powerful moves. Lean in, look into their eyes, let them know: *I care about you.* The person on the other side is not evil and, besides, making that connection more visceral results in great conflict.

And when they are speaking, use these moves to let them know how intently you are listening. It makes those on the other side of the dialogue feel respected and helps them bring their guard down just enough to really hear your words when it's your turn to speak. Getting people to elaborate on a point is another effective way to draw out the truth. People are much less likely to repeat the words of others or be contrived in what they are saying by the third or fourth sentence. When you get them to continue with their stream of words, putting your hand on your chin with those key words and saying, "Tell me more," you get them going, and that's when you get the real story.

Let's say you're having a discussion about trans rights. If the person on the other side of the conversation is a protective father worried about a biological male identifying as a girl using the same locker room as his daughter, the reaction can be visceral. "No way!" he might say. But when they understand better what is going on with an individual who has transitioned from male to female, or female to male, most folks have empathy for someone who has felt trapped in the wrong sex and suffers. You might ask that concerned dad at what age he thinks someone with gender dysmorphia should begin that change through physical appearance and hormone treatments. Or what accommodations should be made in a school setting to make everyone feel safe and accepted? Or what is fair in terms of individual or team sports? Or what the role of a parent, teacher, or guidance counselor should be when a young person gives voice to feelings that suggest transitioning may be a reasonable option? Whatever someone's position on this sensitive issue, there are no easy answers to these open-ended questions. But asking them anyway can yield positive outcomes. There is always at least a sliver of common ground where you can find something you both agree on, which shifts the direction of the conversation toward something more productive. At a minimum, you can walk away feeling like there's room for further discussion, even if you haven't completely changed that person's mind.

The point isn't to demolish the argument so much as to deepen your understanding of the issue. Sometimes the person on the other side of the argument hasn't quite thought something through, but there might be gold if you dig deep enough.

Rather than dismiss something, ask questions to learn more about the thinking that's behind the argument. If you are patient enough to pause, drill down, and understand the intent behind the statement, it can take you in new and unexpected directions.

People are getting stuck in a groove, unable to expand their thinking or change minds because patience and listening have been in short supply, especially lately. Listen to any cable network news show, and on the rare occasion a pundit from the other side of the political aisle is invited for an on-air interview, all you hear is people shouting over each other. Their aim isn't so much to persuade as it is to grind their opponent down.

Cracks and Crevices

The point is to show interest, not judgment. People think they can win conflict by talking over their opponent. But they are handing their adversary the ultimate victory the more they go on, revealing the inconsistencies in their argument. That's why you need to keep them talking. When you hear a flaw in the reasoning that you may be able to counter, mirror what they just said back at them as an innocent question, to get them to clarify. With every sentence or phrase, more information comes out that you may be able to challenge or expand upon. Cracks and crevices start to show through a point that at first seemed solid.

The Dr. Phil Approach

Over the years, Dr. Phil has observed that as I talk to people, I draw them out with questions like "What happened that causes you to have this opinion?" or "And how did that work out for you?" It's not that I am trying to be a therapist, but my techniques aren't far off Dr. Phil's, who asks exposing, probing questions in order to figure out exactly

why people act and think the way they do. My old friend
has taught me a few useful tricks, including paying special
attention to the sentences that follow "but" or "therefore"
because that is where the truth gets told. I do a pretty good
Dr. Phil impersonation and it cracks him up: "*You* know that
I know that *you* know. . . ." Of course, I'm not trying to fix
anyone. I'll leave that to the good doctor. Instead, I'm just
trying to broaden the argument and explore it for holes and
opportunities for us to agree.

I do this all the time on *Bar Rescue*. I'll pick up on something
revealing and mine that vein with the question, "And how do you feel
about that?" or "And how does your wife feel about that?" and so on.
They don't always answer right away. Sometimes you need to let that
long pause do the work for you. When you make a strong point, your
adversary needs that stretch of silence, that interval of space, to let it
sink in. Then, and only then, will they come around, willing to pivot
completely when they've had the opportunity to process the consequences if they don't, and the benefits if they do.

That's what happened on the 100th episode of *Bar Rescue*—"Hard
Heads and Softballs"—when the co-owner of Mac and Chester's SRO
bar in Oak Grove, Minnesota, Todd Chester had a choice: to stop being a drunken man-child or risk bankrupting his family and losing
his wife.

Todd, along with the other owner, Scott Mack, bought the premises because of its huge lot, with four baseball fields, a small bar hut
serving the spectators, and a large bar that served liquor and food to
players and their families after the game. They wanted to turn the old
dive bar around and make it a place where members of the community could come together, and, at first, they did well, netting $800,000
a year.

But then Todd's biker buddies started showing up, intimidating other customers with antics like popping wheelies on the premises and riding their bikes onto tabletops. Todd would cheer them on as they made a ruckus spinning their wheels to make the wood furniture catch fire. The toxicity was causing them to lose $6,000 a month. It got so bad that Scott, once a friend, was done. With his own economic future on the line, they bifurcated the business and Scott was left to run the outdoor business and small concession stand. The feud had literally split the business in half.

Elise, Todd's wife, and mother of his six children, was beside herself. During my recon of the bar, she sat beside me and wept as we watched her drunken husband laughing as his biker buddies turned a picnic table into a bonfire. It was time to get in the man's face.

"She's watching you do these burnouts and applaud," I told Todd, who responded with a smirk.

I decided to wipe that smile off his face.

"So what the fuck are you doing that you think you can make money burning your own furniture?" I yelled. "That is one hundred and fifty dollars you can't give to your own family!"

"Jon, you shut up and listen to me."

"No, you listen to me! You are fucking your family because . . . *Look at me!* You're a fucking idiot . . . !"

Todd lunged for me, and people on set had to pull us apart. I drove away, really not intending to come back except for one reason: Elise. She deserved better.

The next morning, in the sober light of day, I was hoping Todd would come back remorseful. Did he even care? I laid it out for him in the starkest of terms.

"I'm not here to fight with you; I'm here to help you," I told him, then I broke out the numbers. He needed to raise his sales by $30,000 to $40,000 a month to break even. Meanwhile, I added, he was running the place like a basement party. It was hurting Elise and Scott.

"And then you're going to go home and kiss your kids good night. And say, 'Don't worry, I am taking care of you,' and that's a fucking lie, because you're not taking care of them; you're taking care of you. But not really, because you are not going to have a retirement when this is over, and who's the idiot then?"

Then I brought his wife into the conversation.

"I'm exhausted," she confessed to him, tears welling up in her eyes again.

"Todd, she's sinking."

I was speaking just a few inches from his face, sotto voce, and staring straight into his eyes. He went quiet. What you don't see on camera is the long pause, which the producers cut for good television. But that silence works for me. It gives me the opportunity to study someone's reaction. I let my words hang in the air for as long as it takes. They can choose to receive them, or not. After about thirty seconds, with his head bowed in shame, Todd chose wisely.

"She deserves better," he agreed, his voice husky with emotion.

We all agreed that he needed to step back and allow his wife to take the lead. He could go back to doing what he did best: selling real estate. I wasn't expecting Todd to roll over so easily, and neither was he. But as soon as he did, we were able to find a solution for the ownership of the bar, allowing Todd and Elise to buy Scott out. Once we did the makeover, the business boomed. Last I heard it was put on the market for $1 million.

The listening techniques I used with Todd helped to clarify what mattered most to him. He thought it was playtime with his biker buddies, but I came to understand where he truly landed. Watching his reaction—his shame when I played back his behavior to him and his obvious love for Elise—I understood that his desire to take care of his family was his prime motivator, and took the opportunity to remind him of that fact. By discovering what was most important to him, I could emphasize it and move him to do something positive toward that goal. By really listening and engaging, I could sense the change that was taking place in front of me.

Language Barrier

Yolanda Conyers employed these same deceptively simple engagement techniques in a much more complex, international corporate setting, but they were just as powerful. When the Austin-based engineering executive first joined electronics giant Lenovo as chief diversity officer, she was eager to dive in and fix the dysfunction that was plaguing the organization. Maybe a little too eager.

Two years prior, in 2005, Beijing-based Lenovo had inked a historic agreement to acquire IBM's personal computing division, but the Eastern and Western employees who were now forced to work together were struggling to integrate as one company. Lenovo's leadership meant well. Instead of absorbing these different cultures into its own like most acquiring companies do, the goal was to integrate different points of view to create a truly global and unified company. By the time Yolanda was hired, it had infused team members from fifty different countries and multiple corporate cultures. But to say the different groups didn't gel would be an understatement. It was a cacophony of different languages and business protocols, as well as some bad communication habits that both sides needed to quit, fast.

"Screaming doesn't exactly translate well," Yolanda shared with me, referring to some of the Western executives whose aggressiveness backfired during those early meetings.

No one was hearing each other. In response to the chaos, everyone huddled into their own familiar corners, refusing to meet each other halfway. Naysayers were predicting failure. No one believed an East/West merger this ambitious could possibly work.

Understanding the urgency of the situation, Yolanda was on a plane to Lenovo's headquarters within weeks of joining. She'd won awards at her previous employer, Dell, where she was well known for her diplomacy and tact. As Yolanda recounts in her book, "The Lenovo Way: Managing a Diverse Global Company for Optimal Performance,"[1] she felt excited by the challenge she faced, and certain that it was well within her wheelhouse. She spent the next several days interviewing each of the key players one by one, to get to the underlying cause of the conflict. She was pleasant but direct, her usual MO when trying to drill down, gather information, and diagnose a problem. She wished the Chinese team members were a little more forthcoming, but she felt confident they were off to a good start.

Less than twenty-four hours after she flew back to the United States, she heard rumblings that her new colleagues in China were not fans, and that they found her communication style "offensive."

Flabbergasted to learn that she was being viewed as part of the problem she was brought in to fix, Yolanda reached out to one of the Chinese executives with whom she felt she'd struck a rapport—Gina Qiao.

"She didn't say a lot in the group meetings, but when she did, it was meaningful. And there was something about the few times we spoke one-on-one that told me she'd be empathetic," Yolanda recalled.

Gina agreed to meet her for dinner in Hong Kong on Yolanda's next visit. The two women had a long chat about their families, their careers, and what it was like to work as senior executives in a male-dominated industry. They genuinely liked each other and found they had plenty in common. Toward the end of the meal, Yolanda finally mustered the courage to ask Gina where she'd gone wrong.

"It's obvious to me that you are kind and that your intentions are good," Gina told her. "But, from what people are telling me, this is not coming across to our Chinese colleagues at all. In fact, they find you too aggressive. They say that when you ask them a question, you act as if you already know the answer. You don't *listen*."

Gina's words stung. But Yolanda flashed back to all those conversations and realized Gina was right. During all those fact-finding interviews, she'd done most of the talking.

"I must have come across like a bulldozer," Yolanda recalled.

From that point on, Yolanda realized that a big part of her new role would be to listen. She invested more time in getting to know her colleagues better on a personal level. She eventually made the decision to get out of her Western comfort zone and move to Beijing, where she would live for three years with her family. She became more intentional about not putting words in anyone's mouth, even though it might have been tempting to help someone complete a sentence when they seemed to be struggling with the language.

It was incumbent upon Yolanda to allow others time to speak because of the language barrier. Speaking through a translator or exchanging ideas with someone for whom English is a second or third language requires tremendous patience. Words do not always perfectly translate, for example, and it can take several attempts to get the true meaning across. It wasn't unusual for a translator to spend several minutes going back and forth with a Chinese speaker, only to offer up a few words in Chinese, giving Yolanda the impression that more was not being said. But, instead of feeling frustrated, she used that extra time to engage in a more full-bodied version of listening, paying close attention to the body language and vocal tones, which revealed plenty, even if she didn't understand the words. She even encouraged lengthy sidebars, so that the translator and team members could further discuss an issue among themselves, then select someone to speak for the group.

Each time, it was an opportunity to watch, learn, and share the differences on both sides in an effort to bridge the gap. She paid closer attention to the physical tells, like the eye rolls, which happen in every culture, or flushed skin. She took notice when meeting participants turned their chairs away from the table, pulling back their seats and looking off to the side. She observed hand movements— were the hands clasped tightly in their laps or relaxed and loose on the table?

"Sometimes you need to be silent in order to take it all in," Yolanda explained.

Field of Vision

Or, as Tommy "Tony Montana" Mickens put it, "You won't learn anything if you just keep talking."

For Tommy, who was a major drug kingpin in New York City during the 1980s, listening was a matter of life and death. Rappers may have rhymed about Tommy's diamond-encrusted teeth and wristwatches, but the reality of life in the streets of the neighborhoods of Queens, where Tommy had been selling drugs since the age of fourteen, was rife with conflict. His goal was not just to survive in a world where many kids his age were struggling, but to make huge amounts of cash so that he could look after his single mother, support his siblings, and eventually graduate into a legitimate business. Meanwhile, the way to stay ahead of any potential problems and avoid the violence was to maintain relationships with his network of suppliers and customers while keeping the peace with competing dealers and gangs.

Tommy's strategy was to pay close attention to people and his surroundings. Whenever he had to drive somewhere, he says, "I never parked a car head in, so that I could have the full field of vision." When he was involved in a transaction, exchanging marijuana or cocaine for cash, for example, he never allowed anyone to sit behind him in the back seat, because he would be in no position to manage their reactions, much less defend himself if that person decided to put a gun to his head.

"You have to be several moves ahead of someone," Tommy told me. "You have to listen to your instincts, that third eye, tuning into who someone really is so you know what they are thinking and can anticipate what they do next."

Tommy, a master of reaction management, honed his listening skills into a craft. He sat back and let those on the other side of the conversation do most of the talking, "so I could see where they were going with it." He paid attention to those little slips and tells people make in more honest, unguarded moments. He combined his past experiences dealing with different characters around the neighborhood with his own sharp instincts and ability to read body language.

"Things they don't say are just as much part of the conversation," Tommy shared with me. "The person who is quiet, that's who you have to watch."

Engagement with others was an opportunity to gather information that would help him stay ahead of potential threats or rivals to protect himself and achieve his goals. He did not avoid necessary confrontation, but he was cautious and strategic about revealing what he was thinking or allowing himself to react in the moment.

"People fear what they don't understand. Sowing doubt is better than putting on a bulletproof vest, because people don't think twice; they think ten times."

After one too many physical and verbal confrontations as a

teenager, he learned it was sometimes better to give someone else the win, or at least let them think they scored the point. He calls it a mental approach to conflict where you "deal with it, head it off, and engage with them to learn." That knowing and confidence he gains gives him an inner confidence or "aura" that he can project into a room full of strangers, to give him the advantage.

After bringing in as much as $100,000 a week through his drug dealings, Tommy ended his life of crime in 1986, at the age of twenty-two. He had amassed a fortune, including homes around the country, twenty-one luxury cars, and a yacht. 50 Cent glorified Tommy in his song "Ghetto Qu'ran." But, after going legit, Tommy had let his guard down, and two years later he was indicted for drug dealing, money laundering, and tax evasion—nonviolent offenses—and had millions in assets seized. He spent the next twenty years in prison, where conflict was a way of life, and he used the listening skills he'd developed on the streets to survive on the inside.

I share Tommy's story with you because it reveals how leveraging listening in conflict can serve you even in the most precarious situations. Today, Tommy uses his conflict skills for good. After his release from prison, he launched a wellness program, teaching exercise classes for senior citizens, and now he listens to win over others. Tommy, who was his mother's caregiver before she passed from a stroke in 1993, observes and taps into his clients' mood to motivate and inspire, allowing his inner voice to guide him in the service of others. Now he is the legitimate business leader he dreamed of becoming while he was sitting in that jail cell. Not only did Tommy's conflict and listening skills bring him through the other side of a living hell, they gave him the gift of a third act and the chance to give back.

"Forget all those rap songs and riches. This is how I want to be remembered."

Taffer Toolkit Takeaways

1. *Focus on their words, not your next sentence.* If you are constructing that next argument in your head, you're missing some critical information.

2. *Slow it down.* Force yourself to listen. And don't be scared of the silence, because, in constructive conflict, silence can be your friend. Don't be the first person to jump in and lose the point in your eagerness to fill a long pause with words.

3. *Keep them talking.* Utilize encouraging words like "Really?" or "Wow! And?" These terms of engagement will make your adversaries feel good and help you learn the deep-rooted cause of their behavior.

4. *Pay attention to the physical and emotional cues.* There are multiple ways to understand people beyond the words they speak. When you pay attention to these cues, you can control the flow of the discussion.

5. *Employ reaction management.* Shake your head or nod in the direction that you want their views to go, for example. Subliminally, those are powerful moves.

6. *Listen for verbal tells.* The truth often comes out by the third or fourth sentence. Or following the words "but" or "therefore"—according to Dr. Phil!

7. *"So you mean . . . ?"* When you hear a flaw in the reasoning that you may be able to counter, mirror what they just said back to them as an innocent question, to get them to clarify. With every sentence or phrase, more information comes out that you may be able to challenge or expand upon.

8. *Show interest, not judgment.* If you are patient enough to pause, drill down, and understand the intent behind the statement, it can take you in new and unexpected directions. Offer the respect of an open ear.

8

MEET ME ON THE CORNER

It's not just how you engage, but where. Location is another essential tool for constructive conflict.

Years ago, when I was a young man still making my way in the restaurant scene of Los Angeles, I worked at the bar of Barney's Beanery in West Hollywood. Back then, Barney's wasn't the trendy gastropub chain you may recognize today. It was just a small establishment near the Sunset Strip where Quentin Tarantino wrote *Pulp Fiction* from his favorite booth, Oliver Stone filmed scenes from *The Doors*, and everyone from celebrities to street buskers would order its famous chili and burgers. We attracted all kinds of characters, so I wasn't shocked when a gang of bikers, Hells Angels, pulled up front.

These guys weren't bankers out for a weekend joyride in their tricked-out Harleys. They were hardened biker types with long ratty beards and patched leather jackets, and they were thirsty. They ordered a pitcher of beer at the bar and brought it to a table in the adjacent dining room, where they sat down to drink.

The owner came up to me from the back of the house and told me they had to go. It was three o'clock in the afternoon and the place was empty. I didn't think it was the right time to have a conflict with people like this, so I tried another approach. I filled a short glass with beer from the bar, walked over to them, put my glass on their table, pulled up a chair, and sat myself down. They looked up at me, surprised, their arms folded over their hairy tattooed chests.

"Gentlemen, we have a problem," I told them, sotto voce. "You can't be sitting here if you're not eating."

Disarmed as they were by the sheer ballsiness of my move, it was the perfect time to engage. They relaxed their stances and started chatting with me. Then they ordered a couple of snacks, finished their beers, and left peacefully a short time later.

Had I tried to engage with this group before they were all seated, things could have gotten ugly. But by bringing the discussion to them, at their level, where they were relaxing and having a drink, I gained the advantage. Location, location, location!

Depending on who you are meeting in the conflict arena, setting can have a huge impact on the outcome. If your adversary tends to be loud and aggressive, facing that individual down in a noisy sports bar will be far more effective than meeting them at a quiet French bistro, for example. I find sitting down at a table with a Coke is almost always better than standing in the middle of a room, because people are generally calmer and more receptive in that position. But you need to anticipate how the confrontation is going to go down and understand the person on the other side of the conflict.

Other ways to set the stage for the best result include:

- **A long walk or car ride in the country** with your spouse, child, parent, friend . . . True, I advocate eye contact most of the time, but many couples have their best heart-to-hearts, delving deeply into uncomfortable territory, when they are on a long road trip, no distractions and no opportunities to run from each other. With the right person, you can have that difficult conversation while sitting side by side, engaged in activity that doesn't take up too much bandwidth but affords you the opportunity to bring up a sore subject in a way that feels less confrontational. You'd be surprised how much you can hash out when you're in forward motion.

- **A walk around the block of a bar or restaurant** when you want to engage your opponent away from his girlfriend, or out of earshot of her husband, to enable a more honest and open expression of views.

- **In front of a small crowd or just the two of you.** It depends upon how egregious the situation is. Do you want to embarrass this person into doing the right thing, or will the reinforcement of spectators help, or will the fear of spectacle cause your opponent to clam up altogether?

- **An energetic environment like a noisy bar with a beer in hand** to liven up those who are conflict-avoidant and need to come out of their shell. Conversely, if I need someone to be less excitable and more conscious of other people and their surroundings, I might choose to have that heated discussion at a fancy steak house, where there's a murmur of people enjoying themselves in the background and we're dressed up in suits and ties.

Although much of the time we cannot control where conflict happens, because that moment when things come to a head often happens organically, the key is to adjust to the individual and the environment. Respect and understand the setting as well as the player. Depending on whether you are dressed in a ball gown, wearing swim shorts with a piña colada in hand, or on the plant floor in blue overalls, the level of inhibitions will vary. Leverage the situation and location to your advantage. Of course, there will always be moments when the conflict comes to us, even when the setting is less than ideal. That's when you need to be mindful of your surroundings, who is around you, and the potential fallout if things escalate.

Unfriendly Skies

For Kevin, a flight attendant on a popular budget airline, that awareness has become vital to his job performance in an industry plagued with conflict. During 2021, airlines filed 5,114 unruly passenger reports with the U.S. Federal Aviation Administration.[1] Many of the incidents were related to COVID regulations and the mask mandate in flight, but not all. In May 2021, on a Southwest Airlines trip from Sacramento to San Diego, one flight attendant lost teeth and suffered bruises on her face after being assaulted by a passenger who willfully ignored standard flight safety instructions to push up her tray and put her seat back in the upright position.

It's the job of the air crew to be first responders and safety officers on an aircraft, where regulations have tightened on the airways in response to potential threats from terrorism as well as COVID. These conditions have been combined with commercial airlines' decisions to cram in seats and strip down services, forcing flight attendants to do their jobs in an increasingly tense environment, where certain passengers don't take kindly to being told what to do.

The day we spoke, Kevin had just experienced a level of hostility that could have easily gotten out of hand on a flight from San Juan, Puerto Rico, to Fort Lauderdale. As the plane was making its climb to cruising altitude, a gentleman decided to get up out of his seat and grab a bag from his overhead bin.

"Sir, I must ask you to please take your seat," Kevin told him in a polite but firm tone.

But, as the aircraft tilted upward, the man continued to rummage around while standing unsteadily on the tips of his toes.

"Sir, sir! What are you doing?" Kevin asked, getting out of his jump seat and climbing up the aisle toward him.

"What does it look like I'm doing?"

"This is a safety matter. You could hurt yourself and others. Please close the bin and return to your seat. Whatever it is you need can wait until we've finished our ascent and the seat belt sign has been turned off."

Kevin is a big, muscular guy, and this young man didn't appreciate being called out in front of the other passengers, so he took his hostility up a notch.

"I'll take my seat when I want to. Why the fuck are you so rude this morning?"

The irate passenger then took his bag and tossed it at his wife, who was seated next to the window, holding their baby. Horrified, Kevin recognized how easily the situation could escalate, so he took a deep breath, switched gears, and attempted to calm the man down.

"If I have come off as rude, I am sorry," Kevin told him, in a gentler voice. "This isn't about you, or the bag. It is about your safety. You could fall and hurt yourself or someone else. Please just take a seat."

"See! You just admitted that you're rude!" the guy gloated, then, thinking he'd scored a personal victory, sat back down, next to his mortified spouse.

Kevin had no choice but to confront the passenger because his actions were endangering himself and others.

"Up in the air we have few resources and no room to maneuver, so it can be a real shit show. They may think they are in a safe zone, but when that turbulence hits, they could go rolling down the aisle like bowling balls."

But, because of the specific location of the conflict, he knew it was also a matter of safety to deescalate the engagement as quickly as possible. Barroom-like brawls have no place thirty thousand feet up in the air, where two hundred souls trapped in a steel tube have nowhere to run. So, without showing weakness, Kevin made the wise decision to humbly diffuse the situation once it became clear the passenger was going to return to his seat. When he did, Kevin thanked him for cooperating while the man glared back at him. Kevin spent the rest of the two and a half hours ignoring the hothead.

"One of the first things they tell us in training is not to go down to their level," Kevin explained to me. "I can't be the one taking their bait or buying into their drama, so I try to be calm but firm while getting my point across."

At the same time, Kevin can't let certain behaviors slide. Pointing out the dangers of standing up during a climb after the fact would be pointless.

"It's a fine line between laying down the law and triggering a conflict, but I know if I don't inform him of the safety factors and something happens to him, he'll be the first one to complain he wasn't told."

Waiting until the end of a flight to admonish a passenger for failing to comply with a regulation, for example, would also be negligent. "Like not telling your kid what he did wrong when you get home, when it's too far from the moment for the lesson to mean anything," said Kevin. Besides, allowing a passenger to push past the drinks cart to get to the bathroom when the cockpit door is open would be downright reckless.

"I don't know where she'd been since 9/11, but this well-dressed, middle-aged passenger just wasn't getting it," Kevin shared about the time he had to gently but firmly guide a woman back toward the toilets at the rear of the aircraft.

She wasn't happy about it, because they were occupied and it meant she'd have to wait, but Kevin allowed her to vent. He minded his body language and tone, understanding that the teeth sucking and eye-rolling that "some flight attendants are notorious for doing" could ignite a dumpster fire. While he's obligated to lean into a confrontation where there is a safety concern, he tries to be tactful, listening to passengers, communicating clearly, and anticipating their needs and concerns.

"You can never show you're angry, because that's often what they're vying for," Kevin explained. "You try to be discreet and not belittle them in front of the whole plane."

Part of his conflict strategy is to quietly educate. He took the woman aside, into the galley, to give her a quick history lesson on the way airlines protect the cockpit against terrorism threats, using the carts to block the area when the pilot is up and about. (Kevin lost close friends and colleagues on 9/11 for this very reason.) Once she understood, the woman was gracious and apologetic.

During COVID, when seats became unusually cheap and many passengers were first-time fliers, Kevin made no assumptions about their knowledge. He realized many felt irritated, trapped, and uneasy due to a loss of control. Studies have shown that the entire air-travel experience can elevate stress levels in passengers. The Anxiety and Depression Association of America has found that at least 20 percent of Americans are afraid to fly, yet they do anyway, which means more than a handful of people per flight may even be on the verge of a panic attack. So maybe it's understandable that passengers aren't entirely themselves.

Kevin's strategy is to "kill them with kindness" even when the opposite is tempting. He listens, allows them to tell their side of the story, and keeps his voice down. When a conflict erupts, passengers often try to involve their seatmates. They'll point to others whose masks aren't entirely covering their mouth and nose, for example, or start filming scenes on their phones, carefully edited to paint the airline in the worst possible light.

"We are the front line of the company, the image of the brand. Passengers don't remember their interactions with the pilot or gate crew, so it's on us to handle conflict well."

Not that Kevin doesn't have his moments. There are certain boundaries he won't allow to be crossed. Like the time he was pushing the drinks cart down the aisle and felt something sharp digging into his backside. He whipped around to find a woman with three-inch nails as the source of his minor flesh wound.

"Don't do that!" he told her.

"Why, what are you going to do, fuck me up?" she asked with a sneer.

Kevin leaned into where she was sitting and, making sure nobody else could hear, told her with a hiss:

"Do that again and I just might. And I'll make sure the authorities are waiting for you when we land. Never touch someone like that, *especially* during a pandemic."

Thoroughly chastened, the passenger stammered, "Uh, I just wanted a Coke?"

He poured her a cold one and she kept her talons to herself for the rest of the flight.

Crowdsourcing

Of course, the right audience can also foster constructive engagement. Knowing they are being observed by others can often inspire people to be more constructive and accountable in their approach to conflict. They don't necessarily want to look like the bad guy, so they're more self-aware, conducting themselves with decency and listening just a skosh more respectfully to their co-worker, family member, friend, or spouse who might otherwise be on the receiving end of that familiarity which breeds contempt.

When I was filming *Marriage Rescue*, I often found that couples behaved differently toward each other when they knew someone was watching. (The cameras are beside the point—it's surprisingly easy for people to forget they are being filmed.) It wasn't so much that they were pretending as that they were subtly compelled to see themselves and their behavior through the eyes of others. In the same way, we stand up a little taller and cancel the f-bombs when we're interviewing for a job or meeting someone important for the first time. In that moment where these couples are straightening themselves up and noticing who else has entered their space, they get an opportunity to reset their behavior toward each other and treat each other with at least the minimum of dignity and respect they would afford a perfect stranger. Instead of cussing each other out and bickering over every minor thing, something in their brains shifts to the point where they can shut up and listen to each other.

Amber and Riccardo couldn't communicate on any level without bickering. Or I should say, Riccardo could not open his mouth without Amber shouting him down because she was angry. Riccardo had been running up the family debt with his gambling problem, and she kept uncovering these nasty surprises when the overdue charges started showing up in the mail.

The young couple from Atlanta had deeper problems than a gambling addiction, although that was bad enough. It was about trust. She needed an apology from her husband, and the assurance that he'd do better, but she was getting the opposite. The more she yelled, the more he shut down, the more he retreated into himself, the more online gambling or a night at the casino seemed like a great escape. He walked away and played the victim, even though they had kids to support and a mortgage to pay.

"I have to be the hard-shelled man and not the woman in the relationship," she explained.

The result was allowing Riccardo to continuously play the role of victim. He even said their daughter begged them to stop the fighting, giving him the excuse to walk away instead of trying to work out their issues or respond to his wife's complaints.

"You talk, don't listen to anything I have to say, and then tell me I'm lying," he told her.

Their styles of communication were so different, I wondered how the marriage could survive. Amber was an energetic, animated, and communicative young lady who had married a quiet man who held his feelings to himself. She needed to lower the volume and not rise to the point of anger that simply shut him down. And he needed to be more transparent. Riccardo had to commit to telling her what was going on with their finances and knock down that brick wall he'd built up between them.

On every episode, I devise a stress test for each couple. My choice of location is key. Most of the filming takes place at an idyllic beach resort in Puerto Rico, but I wanted these two to get up close and personal with people much less important than themselves. I set them up with a volunteer group to do painting and repairs to the house of a woman named Bianca, who lived in a community that was destroyed by Hurricane Maria. When the pair saw the devastation around them, when they got out of their own heads to pick up paintbrushes and work shoulder to shoulder with Bianca and her family members whose home they were helping to rebuild, you could see their compassion coming to the surface.

Then something interesting happened. The empathy they felt for the people they were helping overflowed toward each other. Suddenly, they were a team, thinking less about their own problems and more about the ways they could help Puerto Rico's distressed families beyond that day. They realized that the financial problems that they were allowing to tear their own family apart were nothing compared to what Bianca and her children were going through.

It was a major breakthrough. The couple recommitted to their partnership. That didn't mean there wouldn't continue to be tense moments in the marriage, because meaningful conflict happens in every important relationship. But at least now they could work toward something as a team. Asking each other to pass the salt no longer had to lead to World War III. They were finally on the same side.

Safe Space

Location doesn't necessarily have to be physical. You can engineer a mindset among people that makes positive engagement possible. You can intentionally create conditions that enable constructive conflict within various teams in a business, for example. A design or creative group might have strong differences of opinion with the sales or accounting people, but the result may actually be better than if either party had their own way. It forces raw talent to hone the product to the point where it makes a profit.

This kind of creative tension defined the relationship between two iconic siblings, Walt and Roy O. Disney, ever since they founded the Disney Brothers Cartoon Studio in Hollywood in 1923. Walt was the guy with the unbridled imagination whose ideas revolutionized the entertainment industry, and Roy, who'd previously worked for a bank in Kansas, was the numbers guy—the pragmatist who kept his younger brother tethered to the earth. Everyone talks about Walt, but, had it not been for Roy, the "happiest place on earth" wouldn't be what it is today.

"If it hadn't been for my big brother," Walt is known to have joked, "I swear I'd have been in jail several times for check bouncing."[2]

One of the most famous conflicts between Walt and Roy occurred during the final edits for *Snow White and the Seven Dwarfs*, which had been the highest-grossing film of all time before *Gone with the*

Wind. But it was also considered one of the most expensive for the age (it was released in 1937) and was dubbed "Disney's Folly." By then they had already spent $1.5 million on a production that was only supposed to cost $500,000. The brothers had mortgaged themselves to the hilt and sold everything: their homes, their furniture, their art collections. . . . But they still needed to fix two cells that had been out of sequence, causing the prince's body to flicker during the kissing scene. They were broke, and it would have cost thousands more to fix.

"Let the prince shimmy!" Roy told them.[3]

Who knew it wasn't a designed effect? But, as far as the audience was concerned, that fiscal decision made a pivotal scene in the movie even more magical. Forced to work within the limits of business considerations, the creative result was even better than Disney's artists might have produced otherwise. The movie grossed an initial $8 million and won an Academy Award.

Roy and Walt were known for having many conflicts about dollars and creativity during their lives, but that conflict yielded some of the greatest creative yet financially sound results in history. Ideas get refined through creative tension, which almost always results in a better product.

Of course, that tension could only exist without destroying the partnership because of the unconditional and loving space that existed between Walt and Roy. Even though Roy was eight years older, the two were extremely close, and even shared a room in their humble Midwestern home.

"We had to sleep in the same bed," Roy recalled many times. "Walt was just a little guy, and he was always wetting the bed. And he's been peeing on me ever since."[4]

But Roy gave whatever he had to support his brother's dreams, raising money from friends and family members because he believed in Walt's vision. Like the time, in 1928, when they needed a small fortune to pay for the extra music recording costs of *Steamboat Willie*—the movie that was arguably the debut of Mickey and Minnie Mouse. The brothers had already leveraged everything they had, and not for the last time. Roy financed the added production cost by selling Walt's beloved 1926 Moon Roadster while his brother was in New York working on the soundtrack. Imagine how Walt must have felt coming home to an empty garage. But he had no choice. Beyond the $5,000 or so in production costs, there was also payroll to be met, among other accounts payable.

Roy was all in because he understood how revolutionary this animated short would be. It was to be the first cartoon with fully synchronized sound, including a bouncing ball to keep up the tempo (this was at a time before most of you were born, when talkies had only recently taken over from silent films). But production of the animated short was fraught with obstacles and unexpected costs. This was brand-new technology that required some trial and error to finesse. Some of the animators didn't even believe it would work.

Before the final sound values were added, Walt and Roy staged a screening for the studio staff and their families, who sat in the office next to Walt's. They wanted to be certain it was worth all that financial risk. Roy placed a movie projector outside, in front of the window, so that the whirring noise from the machinery wouldn't mess with their improvised sound effects, which included someone playing the mouth organ, while others played slide whistles and banged on spittoons, pots, and pans. Walt provided the minimal dialogue, grunts, and laughs. The audience was captivated.

Creative Tension

Roy did a lot more than just make sure his brother had enough money for his projects. Always thinking ahead, he maximized their profits

and protected his brother's copyrights in court. Roy set up a lucrative merchandizing business, licensing rights for Mickey and other
characters to toys, games, books, etc. for what would eventually rake
in more than $100 billion in annual sales. Walt, for his part, helped
his brother see the future with technologies like Technicolor and, of
course, those wild rides in Disneyland.

But, over the years, the tightfisted Roy and the dreamer Walt had
some conflict doozies. Creative tension would be a gross understatement. The more successful they got, and the more successes that were
at stake, the worse it got. At one point Disney was effectively two
companies. Separate from the animation studio, Walt had founded
Walter Elias Disney (WED—the forerunner of Imagineering) to
oversee Disneyland. Fearing that Walt's spin-off company could become an issue for shareholders, Roy acquired WED, to reunite his
brother with the studio, but it led to a raging argument about Walt's
compensation. The two men reportedly had a shouting match that
lasted for three straight days.

Months later, as Walt's contract was about to expire and there
was a real threat of the co-founder leaving Disney altogether, tense
legal negotiations ensued, and things were at a standstill. But big
brother had had enough. He walked into the conference room and
announced to his team of lawyers:

"None of us would be here in these offices if it hadn't been for
Walt. All your jobs, all the benefits you have, all came from Walt and
his contributions. He deserves better treatment than what's being
shown here."[5]

They reached a deal and, according to Disney historian Theodore
Kinni, Walt showed up for Roy's next birthday carrying a Native
American peace pipe.

"Perhaps because they had come so near to losing each other,

Roy and Walt seemed closer than ever after the reconciliation. They worked together for the rest of their lives," Kinni writes.[6]

Where It's Safe to Disagree

Of course, creating a safe space in which to have these discussions takes leadership. Say, for example, a company's marketing team came up with an ad campaign that's genius but way over budget. It's a situation that could easily lead to a clash of priorities. But it doesn't necessarily have to be that way. Employees, no matter their role in an organization, need to know their leaders care about what they think. It's also incumbent upon management to make people feel comfortable enough to disagree with one another—even their bosses!

That level of trust doesn't necessarily come in an instant, so it's important to do some ground setting and charter building before you engage. Ensure that everyone agrees on certain priorities, to which everyone can return whenever the discussion veers. Even if your colleagues can't align on the details of how to get there, they can agree on the intention, or the destination if not the road map.

To that end, if you are running a meeting you may want to consider announcing at the beginning that constructive conflict will be embraced. Let them know there are no bad ideas, and everyone's input will be treated with respect, although it will also be put to the test. Whatever happens in the room will ultimately lead to a better place. People may get upset, because everyone is passionate about their work, but that it's all in service of the mission. One executive I know who works for a consumer brand often asks her team:

"Does anyone believe they can create the best thing from one person's opinions?"

Of course, the answer is always no.

She uses provocative questions to ground people in what they are doing. She also splinters off members of the team into smaller groups, or what she calls "feeder meetings," so that less forthcoming, or shy, folks feel more comfortable about getting their ideas on the table.

"People are wired in different ways; you can't allow the type As to overtake," she explained to me. "You must pull it out of the quiet members of the group or risk missing out on the prize."

It takes emotional intelligence to lead through the creative tension. If someone is upset and starts shouting when they experience pushback on an idea, perhaps allow them to blow up, on the understanding that they'll come around eventually. Maybe they just need to sleep on it. Give them time rather than force it, and let the germination process occur.

Again, as Walt and Roy often found, creativity constrained by financial limits often results in a much better product—something much more imaginative than when they started. The business pressure spurs creativity. When the idea doesn't measure up to the overall mission, which, after all, is to make a profit, everyone digs a little deeper.

This approach to conflict would work just as well in a family discussion or a disagreement between spouses. Agree on the mission, hash out the ideas, test them, and allow each other to come to the solution at their own pace. But what if your workplace isn't a safe space that welcomes diverse thought or challenges to the status quo? What then?

Short answer: you are probably screwed.

Uneven Playing Field

Life is about power imbalances. Like it or not, it behooves you to have a sense of your place in the pecking order before you decide to engage in a conflict. When I was a child, my mom was the boss of me. As I cowered in the basement, she could make or break me, literally. At school, my teachers were the boss. When I tended bar, the proprietor who signed my paychecks had the power. In the workplace, unless you're the owner of the business, there are people all around you who can determine if you're going to have a good day, or a bad one. Even the owner may have to answer to the bank or some investors.

It's always going to be an uneven playing field everywhere you turn. That's why I've been in the process of creating a show called *Beat the Boss*—a kind of Dr. Phil–format show filled with a studio audience that forces small and medium business owners and their people to confront their dysfunction. On *Bar Rescue*, the operational problems are almost always the result of a troubled owner projecting their garbage onto their staff. Nothing infuriates me more than seeing a person in power bully or belittle the people beneath them, so this show gives me a chance to be the advocate for the underdog, empowering them to confront rather than tiptoe around the conflict.

But unless you have someone like me in your corner—a third party willing to drill down to the truth and shame a boss who is abusing power—you will need to make that quick calculation I discussed in chapter 3. This is where it is critical to pick your battle. Before you speak truth to power, which I am all for, you must decide what your end goal is, and whether it is worth losing that income or position. What, realistically, is the risk-to-reward ratio? It may not come to it and, with the aid of internal champions within the organization, like a mentor or a supportive team leader, you may well be able to engage in the conflict and get yourself heard with a positive outcome. The issue you address with your superior may even save the business or make working life more bearable for the rest of your downtrodden colleagues. But it may not, in which case you need to be okay with walking away.

Louisa was fine with that. She'd already decided she'd had enough with the large overseas news bureau where she'd been working for the previous ten years. She was tired of how political the place had become. People who were playing the game rather than producing groundbreaking, investigative journalism were getting ahead, while the old-school reporters were being left behind. The business had changed, and now it was all about clickbait and putting forth political biases instead of impartially uncovering the facts.

Newsroom Brawl

She could have stayed at the newspaper a little longer. As much as she hated the politics, there were still one or two stories she wanted to write, and she liked having that news organization's resources enough to tolerate the BS. But she reached a tipping point when a junior editor, Hank, decided to junk up one of her stories with unsubstantiated embellishments and claims. It wasn't the first time he tried to make his mark as an editor, but this crossed the line. When he sent the article back to her, she diplomatically pointed out the problematic edits, which set off a back-and-forth that grew increasingly contentious. Finally, she was done.

"Okay, Hank, if you want to run the story your way, that's fine. Just take my name off it."

"What? You can't do that!" he yelled in the middle of the newsroom. "This story needs a byline and that's on you!"

"You cannot publish something under my name that I disagree with so no, Hank, it's on you. Stick your name on the byline. In fact, you can stick it altogether."

"How dare you say that to me!" he said. "I am your editor! I outrank you!"

By this time, everyone in the open-plan newsroom was staring. Emboldened, Hank started accusing her of being "a difficult woman" who was "unwilling to be a team player." By loudly pulling rank in front of a captive audience, Hank thought he could shame Louisa into submission. He had no idea she'd already made up her mind.

"Sorry, bud. You're nothing but a glorified desk grunt who can't string a grammatical sentence together. You have no news judgment, you are reckless, and you don't outrank me because I quit!"

That's one way to win a workplace conflict. Put yourself in a position where you have nothing to lose and, yes, you *can* have the last word. Louisa could take that final, principled stand because she'd already considered what could happen and had been anticipating just such a scenario for months. She never learned if her conflict moved the needle forward for the quality of journalism at the paper, or the way her fellow reporters might also be treated in that hierarchical environment, but it sure felt good to stand up for her principles.

We all have the power of individual choice when faced with conflict, whether it's through leveraging location, creating safe spaces for constructive engagement, or acknowledging where you exist on the food chain and what you are willing to risk when you take your stand against The Man. Having that sense of place is another tool, enabling you to position yourself accordingly.

But there is one place where there is no risk/reward for engagement: the internet. Conflict on social media is worthless. Hiding behind a screen gives people a false sense of empowerment—a feeling that they can hurt or cancel you while their anonymity protects them from any consequences. Then things go viral, and the online peanut gallery takes over.

Why not avoid that virtual bust-up altogether? Do you even want your beliefs to be taken and twisted in the echo chambers of Insta-gram, Twitter, Facebook . . . ? Because all that digital drama is not real. If you just cannot help yourself, the best solution for a crowd attack is to herd everyone. If the mob disagrees with something you said, enlist others on social media to fight for you. Ask them what they think. Get a crowd discussion going and then take a step back from it so that you don't have to be the target. If you do find yourself bearing the brunt of it, don't apologize and don't engage. Just wait thirty-six hours for the virtual mob to move on.

That's how I handled the Twitter frenzy after an appearance in 2016 on *The Meredith Vieira Show*, when Meredith asked me to mix her a drink.

"You know, my husband says I make the worst Manhattan in the world," she told me as we walked from the studio couch to the bar.

The problem was that her producers had stocked the bar with in-gredients for an old-fashioned, the cocktail I'd been originally in-structed to make. I figured she must have misspoken and I didn't want to correct her on live television, so I did my best, even though a Manhattan's key ingredient is vermouth, which wasn't there.

You would not believe some of the hate-filled messages on social media. "Jon Taffer of *Bar Rescue* Makes the Worst Manhattan" blared a headline on Reddit.[7]

I did not respond, and the twit storm went away in a day.

This book is not about online conflict. Attacks on social media are not relevant. Cloaked behind the screen, people can say what-ever illogical thing they want without consequence. They must be dismissed. They are not worth the waste of mental energy. Do me the honor of showing up for the discussion face-to-face and I'll be glad to engage with you anytime, anywhere.

Taffer Toolkit Takeaways

1. *Match the location to the adversary.* Anticipate how the confrontation is going to go down and understand the person on the other side of the conflict. Respect and understand the setting as well as the player.

2. *Be hyper-aware of your surroundings.* There will always be moments when the conflict comes to us, even when the setting is less than ideal. Know who is around you and the potential fallout if things escalate.

3. *Crowdsource.* The right audience can foster constructive engagement. Knowing they are being observed by others can often inspire people to be more constructive and accountable in their approach to conflict.

4. *Location isn't just physical.* Engineer a mindset among people that makes constructive engagement possible. Intentionally create conditions—safe spaces—that allow for constructive conflict.

5. *Know your place.* Understanding where you stand on the food chain can be another tool, enabling you to position yourself accordingly.

6. *In-person only.* Conflict on social media is worthless. Hiding behind a screen gives people a false sense of empowerment—a feeling that they can hurt or cancel you while their anonymity protects them from any consequences. Never let that happen. Within days, the peanut gallery will have moved on anyway.

9

BE THE BRIDGE

*Forcing conflict can bring people closer. Seek the
healing power of a good old-fashioned dustup,
with some ground rules. . . .*

Juan Pablo was behaving like a dog. He and his wife, Edith,
had owned a bar in Orange County, California—La Luz Ultra
Lounge—that had been failing for years. They had three kids together and were thousands of dollars in debt. As is often the case,
their business problems were mere symptoms of the broken relationships in the family. But Juan Pablo was too busy chasing women and
treating his wife and kids like crap to notice.

By the time I met the couple, Edith was getting ready to leave and
divorce Juan Pablo. I didn't blame her. It was clear the relationship
was circling the drain. But something told me the relationship could
still be salvaged, so I decided to try something. I brought Edith into
my car to review security footage during the preshow recon of the
bar, as we do during every episode. That's when we saw Juan Pablo
in the bar as a pretty young lady walked up to him and asked if he
was married, to which Juan Pablo replied, "There's no ring on this
finger."

It was painful to watch. Edith completely lost it. In between sobs, she told me how her husband never comes home at night, that he's a womanizer, that he's running the family business into the ground, leaving his children with nothing.

"Edith, listen to me," I told her. "When you walk into that bar tonight, your husband has to think that this is a new day, that you are not going to tolerate this anymore. And for the first time ever, I'm here. I've got your back."

Edith nodded, trembling and clenching those divorce papers tight in her fist. But she'd made up her mind to serve him, like she'd done so many other times before, so I wasn't done.

"But if he thinks that you are going to let this slide tonight, like you have every other night, this does not end, do you get that? You need to go in there and you need to make a statement that this is enough!"

Edith got out of my SUV and charged into the bar, with me following close behind her. Without missing a beat, she smacked her philandering husband right on the mouth, ripped his shirt off, and dumped a drink, ice cubes and all, onto his chest.

Caught completely off guard, Juan Pablo protested as if he were the innocent victim. That's when I called him a fool and a cheater. He was a big guy, but he didn't try to lunge at me, so I kept going, making him face all the ways he'd screwed over himself, his wife, his family, and his business. He had no words to defend himself. Then something extraordinary happened. He started crying genuine tears of remorse.

By the time the episode was over, Juan Pablo and Edith's marriage was on its way to healing. Edith tore up the divorce papers. The two started working together as a team, respecting each other and tending to their neglected business. At the end of filming, Juan Pablo handed me a letter that read, *You were the father that I never had. Nobody ever spoke to me that way.*

This marriage was crying out for a confrontation. I had attacked the man more aggressively than anyone had ever attacked him in his life. Together with Edith, I made him look at himself in a whole new way. And everything in that couple's world turned around because someone had the courage to confront him. That's how desperately Juan Pablo needed the honesty.

Keep It Real

At the end of every *Bar Rescue* episode but one, I've gotten a hug from the very people I've told to go fuck themselves. I am convinced that it's because they were crying out for an honest confrontation. They needed someone to make them hear the truth and hold them accountable for it. They needed me to be that bridge, that agent for honest communication, to bring them closer with their loved ones, their business partners, and their associates.

Of course, the usual ground rules of respect and finding common ground apply. Chances are, if you are trying to force the confrontation, it is because you care deeply about this person. But that is why it's paramount that you don't let your adversary off the hook. You owe it to both yourself and the person you are in conflict with to keep it real. Here's how:

Explain—Don't complain. Complaining to or about your conflict or your adversary may make you feel good by relieving some of the frustration you feel, but it is not a winning tactic for resolving conflict. Complaining adds no value to a disagreement and, in fact, can inhibit your opponent's willingness to listen to and possibly accept your view. Complaining is redundant where there is conflict, so get past it fast and put your focus where it should be: on the substance of your argument. Only then can you move an adversary to embrace it. Conflict is typically won on positive factors that bring beneficial things to life, business or otherwise. Complaining does not win conflicts. Complaining does not gain respect. Why are you right . . . not, why are they wrong?

Skip the Apologies. Conflict is a tool to an end. In and of itself, positive conflict requires no apology. Never say you're sorry for what you believe or who you are; passion and conviction require no apology. Only anger requires an apology. A powerful byproduct of meaningful conflict (win or lose) is the opportunity to show one's knowledge, integrity, purpose, maturity, and other attributes or skills. The confidence and ability to engage in positive and meaningful conflict, even if it does not change minds, creates respect and adds to one's perception of character. Those with the apparent confidence to speak their minds and engage in smart, positive conflict are perceived as strong, go-getters, and contributors. Their willingness to step up garners respect.

Bringing about the right conditions to call someone on their harmful, self-destructive BS is my whole mission. Making an individual confront the truth in real time is that first all-important step toward growth because, until it happens, until they can really hear you, that point of contention is always going to fester. It will be the cancer that kills the business, ruins the marriage, causes estrangement in the friendship, or creates the dysfunction in your family that messes up the kids for life. So, in many ways, forcing conflict is an act of love.

Of course, you need to be delicate about it. You can't just set off a bomb, sit back, and watch the fallout. Just as yelling is a specific technique that can force your adversary to wake up and face a truth, a combination of conflict techniques is necessary to create the right conditions to bridge that chasm in a relationship. It's not enough to be willing to step in and knock heads together. This is where you bring into play all the Taffer conflict tools you've been reading about up until now, from strategically raising and lowering the volume to full-bodied listening, to finding common ground. Forcing the kind of engagement that heals requires plenty of compassion and emotional intelligence.

Broadwalk Blues

That EQ was badly needed during the filming of *Bar Rescue*'s Season Four episode "Beach Rats." We went to recon a bar/restaurant on the boardwalk of Hollywood, Florida, about forty minutes north of Miami called Toucan's Oceanside Bar and Grill. This place should have been a gold mine. It was a spacious corner lot right on the beach, with daily foot traffic of thousands of tourists along its boardwalk, which is called the "Broadwalk." All the nearby establishments were bustling, but Toucan's was completely empty right at the time most bars would be filling up for happy hour. Something was seriously wrong with the place, but it sure wasn't the location. I could not imagine why an asset like this would be failing.

Instead of sending someone else in, I decided to do a recon in person this time. I walked in with my team—chef Nick Liberato and mixologist Kyle Mercado—and we ordered every drink on the menu. Even though we were the only people in the place, it was a struggle to get the attention of the bartender, Kali. When she finally shuffled over, she didn't even have a pad to write down our orders. It felt like she was annoyed to have customers interrupting her day. Then, when she served our drinks, it was clear she was just guessing how to make certain cocktails. Even worse was the food. We ordered some oysters, which you would expect to be good when you're dining by the ocean, but they were covered with barbecue sauce and grit. Completely inedible.

I thought a few more customers might help get them going, so

I rounded up about sixty people from the boardwalk, giving them a chance to make some money. The owners were about $250,000 in debt, having sunk in all their retirement savings, and they were continuing to lose about $8,000 a month. If they didn't get their revenues flowing again, they had about five months before they'd have to shutter. But the experiment failed. Toucan's staff was so overwhelmed that Kali couldn't even ring the drink orders through and ended up giving $2,000 worth of liquor away. Logan, the cook, walked off the job. Meanwhile, we discovered that the kitchen was coated in grease and filth, there were bugs inside the liquor bottles, and there was black mold by the draft beer taps. These were major code violations. I had to shut the place down.

Under these circumstances, I'd normally walk away. I can't afford to be involved in a business that serves food and drink that could make people sick. The risk to my professional reputation is too great. But there was something about the two owners, Jamie Hawkes and his longtime best friend, John Franke, that told me lack of care and leadership wasn't the whole story here. When they first arrived from New Jersey ten years earlier, their bar was hopping. They'd been scrappy enough to survive damage from two major hurricanes, building back better and stronger each time. So what happened? Their staff had turned sour and unmotivated for a reason. I needed to dig deeper to find out what was really going on.

On the condition that they did a deep clean, I agreed to come back three days later and try again. Nick and Kyle gave them some new food and cocktail recipes, in addition to some training and motivating of the staff. This time we brought 120 people into the bar. It was hopping, but the kids were catching up with the orders and executing them well. I was pleased, until Nick felt the pitter-patter of little feet between his legs as he was working in the kitchen. The place was infested . . . with rats!

Again, we shut it down. I collared Jamie and told him, "This is on you. Have you not heard of corporate responsibility?"

Rats are a well-known hazard in tropical climates, especially on a boardwalk, and anyone with a business, especially one that serves food and beverages to customers, must invest in regular extermination. The fact that the place had been infested was the ultimate sign he'd let everything go to shit.

"I had a rough year," Jamie told me.

"So what? " I replied. "I had a rough year too. I've been through many of the same issues as you."

"Did your son die?" he asked me.

There it was. The root cause. Jamie was in the depths of grief, it was affecting everyone and everything around him, and he did not know how to climb his way out.

"What was his name?" I asked him.

"Jamie," he told me, pulling a chain with dog tags out from under his shirt, one with a photo of his beloved boy, and another with the words *Forever in My Heart*.

James "Jamie" Hawkes IV had been murdered less than a year prior, in December 2013. He'd been living in Independence, Oregon, and working undercover as an informant for the narcotics team of the Polk County police department. Jamie was beaten to death by two drug dealers who had somehow found out he was working with the cops, and his body was found near a cemetery. I'm no stranger to loss, but nothing like that. As a parent, I can't imagine what it must have been like to lose a child, especially in such a sudden, brutal, and unjust way. No wonder all the spirit had drained out of the place.

Jamie's way of coping was to pour himself into the day-to-day operations of the business, but not in a good way. He was angry and unfocused. He gave inconsistent direction to his employees, then berated them when they couldn't read his mind. He treated his partner the same way. Once best friends, they were no longer on speaking terms. They rotated eighteen-hour shifts so they never had to be in the same room together, because when they were, they'd cuss each other out. They had already been exhausted from the long hours and pressure before Jamie's son died—to the point where both of their wives walked out on them. But since the tragedy, things had spiraled. And in the process, the owners had grown to hate each other.

I had to fix this relationship somehow. If these two old friends couldn't make things work, if they couldn't come back together as a team, all my efforts to revive their bar would be wasted. The business would surely fail. After all that they'd put into the place, Jamie and John would end up broke and alone.

The next morning, I called the two men to the bar.

"I know that this has been hard for you to talk about, I know he wasn't your son, but you think of him too, don't you?" I asked John.

"Every day," he said. "Everybody died a little inside when it happened."

"It made you deal a little bit differently with Jamie, didn't it?"

"I think so."

"I want you guys to start communicating with each other like you used to. John, what is it that you need to say to Jamie to open this up again?"

"Well, all I can say is that we need to start everything over now. It's a new day. If we work closer and can all be on the same page, that will help one hundred percent."

That was it. John identified the solution. But now I had to make Jamie *want* that new day.

"Look at what you've lost," I told them. "If you lose each other, too, it'd be over, wouldn't it?"

They both nodded in agreement. They knew what was at stake.

"Jamie, I have a hard question to ask you. When does the mourning end, and life begin again?"

He started crying. So did John. So did I.

"You can have a brand-new business, you can have a whole new future. . . . Isn't it time to step up in his memory?" I asked Jamie.

"Yeah," he said, barely able to get the word out as he choked back his tears.

"Rather than shut down in his memory?"

"Yeah!" he answered, with more conviction this time. Then, looking up, he whispered, "I just want him to sit there and say, 'We did it!' And I hope you're peaceful, Jamie. . . ."

"Tell him what it's time to do," I told him. "You need to say it and he needs to hear it."

"Gotta move on . . . gotta move on," he said, then buried his face in his hands, sobbing. "God, it fucking hurts!"

The entire film crew was bawling by this point. It was by far one of the most emotionally challenging moments in the history of the show. And the most gratifying. As soon as I was able to get this bereft father to see what his pain was doing not just to him, but to others, everything changed. Making him realize that he wasn't alone, and that others truly shared his grief, was another catalyst for positive change. You could feel the energy in that bar lighten.

We gave the place the usual face-lift. We renamed the bar Bonny and Read's Toucan Hideout, to commemorate two badass female pirates who used to sail to this part of South Florida as their safe haven. Immediately, customers started flocking to the place, and the revenues were more robust than ever. But the real shift was in Jamie and his partnership, or I should say brotherhood, with John.

This is the kind of healing that conflict can bring. When you force someone to confront the truth, you can crack them open just wide enough that they can receive. But it needs to be done with the utmost care. If you watch the episode, you'll notice I never once yelled at the owners. I was uncharacteristically low-key, because that technique would not have accomplished my goal with Jamie, which was to gently guide him out of that deep, dark hole he was in. I wanted to be that bridge that would help him cross from a state of grief to a mindset of wanting to live.

Cathartic Confrontations

There are so many situations where it is impossible to move forward without the willingness to have a difficult conversation. These cathartic confrontations can save businesses, relationships, and lives. Without these open and honest dialogues as a society, we are sunk. As individuals, the unwillingness to face conflict leaves us stuck in mindsets and behavior that don't serve us. To bring about the dialogue, to utter some uncomfortable truths that can bring greater clarity, understanding, or closure, you must force yourself to go there, or at least find someone willing to do it for you.

Pamela Slaton, an investigative genealogist who makes a living finding, and often reuniting, birth parents with the biological children they gave up for adoption, has these kinds of conversations on a regular basis. She is the one who must make that phone call to a birth parent she has confirmed and tracked down through multiple pieces of evidence and official records. By the time she picks up the phone, there is no doubt in Pamela's mind that the person on the other end of the conversation is the mother, father, child, or sibling of her client who is searching.

But Pamela is also aware that the individuals she reaches out to are not necessarily prepared for the call, which can trigger all kinds of past trauma. A birth mother often feels guilty and, in some cases, fearful of her spouse or family members finding out. The reality of a birth child coming back into their lives digs up long-buried pain, shame, and heartbreak. Many of these adoptions took place long ago, when it was common for an unwed mother to go into hiding when she began to show, giving birth in another town so that her condition could remain a secret.

Pamela first puts herself in that person's shoes, telling the birth mother:

"I realize this is not a call you are expecting, but I am helping someone find their family. They've done the DNA and I would like to speak about the search I am doing."

After a few beats of silence, that person will either be in shock, denial, or relief that this day has finally come. She pays attention to the tone of their voice to determine "if I have to coddle or be a badass."

"If you can't do this and no one in your family knows, I understand the shame and times when you had this child," she tells them. "I am an adoptee myself."

If they put up resistance, she often urges them to at least take the opportunity to wish their biological child the very best.

"Please say something so that the last memory they have of you is of you saying something kind," she suggests. "Give them the chance to say thank you for giving them life. What is the harm in one conversation?"

These folks usually come around once they've had a chance to digest the news, but not always. Pam pushes hard for these conversations because she knows it will make the lives of both parties better in some way, whether that's something as profound as helping to lighten the burden of guilt of the birth parent, or simply giving her client access to relevant family medical history. Sometimes there's a longing to connect that was pushed aside because the parent or child never believed it was possible. Sometimes not.

One elderly Irish woman kept denying what Pamela had to tell her.

"Hey, I understand," Pamela told her. "You're panicking now because you're in shock. But I want you to know that the records will be opened because an attorney will get involved. Right now the situation is confidential and controlled, but once the court's involved, let me tell you what's coming down the pike. . . ."

A couple of days later, the woman called Pamela back, annoyed.

"Yeah, okay, I'm the mother. What now?"

Her daughter contacted her and they met for lunch at a hotel in New York City. The two women chatted for three hours. Afterward, Pam's client called her to say she wasn't a fan of her birth mother. All she did was talk about herself. It was clear she was just there to tell her story so that her birth daughter would stop pestering her and go away. But that selfish attitude was a gift in and of itself. Pamela's client was thankful that her birth mother gave her up for adoption, and even more appreciative of her adoptive mother.

"At least they got some kind of closure," Pamela explained.

One Muslim mother got a relationship she'd been longing for but never dared believe possible. If her husband and extended family ever got wind of the fact she'd had a child out of wedlock, it could have destroyed her. Culturally, she could have been cut off, or worse. She kept aggressively denying the truth, until Pamela changed tact and said, "So let me ask you something: Do you ever think of this girl?"

The woman started sobbing. "Not a day goes by when I don't think of her."

"Then help me to help you to figure out how to make this work."

She set up a PO Box, and the mother and daughter have been pen pals ever since.

Healing was the goal when Pamela had to initiate the most difficult of conversations with a mother who had given up her baby after being beaten and raped at a young age. Uncertain how she was going to react to the reminder of this horrific event in her life, Pamela called the woman's sister first. The sister then broached it with her sibling, who wanted to speak with Pamela directly. When the woman picked up the phone, her first words were:

"I always thought this day was going to come."

"I hope and pray you'll consider the fact that your biological son is blameless," Pamela told her. "He was part of a crime committed, but I firmly believe he was meant to be on this earth."

"I cannot agree more," the woman replied. "I think of him every year. I am terrified but would love to speak with him."

Pam the Payloader

Make no mistake, these interactions stir up more than heartache. Some birth relatives are infuriated by what they see as an intrusion, and they project all their fear and resentment onto her as the messenger. Pamela gets threats of lawsuits, even death, for trying to initiate these conversations. One man sent her a stream of angry emails.

I'm going to track you down, he wrote.

But Pamela is as unapologetic as she is unrelenting.

"Please consider what I have to say to the person on the other end of this situation," she told one reluctant birth dad. "Do you want me to say you don't care and never thought of this person? Is that really what's in your heart? Or can we come to some sort of agreement to end things on a positive note?"

In Pamela's field, the hard fact of DNA results can help people to face reality. After jumping through hoops to prove one gentleman was the birth father to three young women, he finally agreed to meet them in person. But at the last minute he backed out of the gathering, claiming he wasn't sure he was their father. He didn't want to confront his past as a teenage Lothario and the possibility his offspring might accuse him of being a deadbeat, so he clung to the uncertainty.

The girls were heartbroken, and Pamela was annoyed. After multiple attempts, she finally convinced him to take the DNA test "just to rule it out." Of course, he was their dad, and the reunion finally happened.

"I'm the one who shoves the proof in their faces. I'm the payloader," Pamela joked.

Her own adoption story did not have the same satisfactory ending. Instead, it was a painful beginning. Growing up, she'd fantasized about the type of woman her birth mother was. She had loving adoptive parents, and she grateful that her birth mother, Lucille, just a teenager at the time, had had the courage and wherewithal to find her a good family. From her teens, Pamela had made several attempts to track her down without success. The urge to find her only increased when she was married and pregnant with her first child, eager to learn more about her firstborn son's lineage. She started sleuthing again, and soon pieces of the genealogy puzzle came together. She'd found Lucille's number and gave her a call.

"Yeah, sure, I'm your mother," Lucille told her, in a tone so corrosive, it could have stripped paint. "And guess what, your father is *my* father. Never call me again!"

Pamela was devastated. For months after that call, she had panic attacks. Lucille's cruelty made her question everything she thought she knew about herself. But it also inspired Pamela to launch her career as a searcher, having discovered she was a natural detective. She was determined to prove Lucille wrong and find out who her father really was (and no, it wasn't her grandfather). She also believed that, by bringing about positive reunions for others, she could heal through their joy. She was right on both counts.

About twenty-five years later, out of the blue, Lucille knocked on Pamela's front door. Pamela came face-to-face with a tall blond-haired, blue-eyed woman who looked exactly like an older version of herself. She was shaking at the thought of confronting a woman who'd brought her so much pain, but she invited her into her home, and the two sat together in Pamela's backyard for the next seven hours, sharing their lives with each other, laughing, crying, and cursing. Pamela got her chance to tell Lucille how aggrieved she felt, and Lucille got her opportunity to explain herself. It wasn't perfect, but it paved the way for forgiveness and "the next day I woke up feeling so much lighter," Pamela recalled. "I had to wait long enough [more on that in chapter 10], but the conflict that plagued me my whole life was finally resolved."

That conversation was further confirmation that even the most difficult interactions are worth the pain. This is especially true in Pamela's business, where the conflict is layered through some of the most fundamental questions human beings can have about their identity—how they came into this world.

"People are not always conceived in the best of circumstances," Pamela shared with me. "Birth parents carry that shame, and their children carry the burden of their conception, on their backs, whether they are the byproduct of rape, incest, neglect, or abandonment. Neither side wants to be the cause of pain or the object of hatred. No parent-and-child relationship should be shoved into the darkness like the family sin."

That's why Pamela's whole purpose is to bring about the kinds of constructive engagements that help her clients understand that the circumstances of their birth are no fault of theirs, nor are they responsible for the actions of their birth parents. She won't quit until she tracks down the other party and makes the connection, because she knows firsthand how cathartic it can be for everyone involved. And if she irritates someone along the way, so be it.

"You have to be badass and ballsy to have these conversations," Pamela told me. "But that is exactly what I was put on this earth to do."

Acquisition Angst

Of course, forcing conflict is not only healthy for personal relationships. The willingness to lean into tough conversations can make or break a business, sometimes with billions of dollars at stake. Think about all those failed mergers. According to most studies, up to 90 percent of corporate acquisitions fail,[1] costing billions in lost productivity and opportunity costs, not to mention jobs. A big reason for these failures comes down to the inability to integrate the cultures of the companies, particularly when they are global and management is not only trying to blend different internal corporate cultures, but entirely different national identities, languages, and cultural norms.

The result is a series of culture clashes that can lead to a lack of trust and an inability to communicate past the false assumptions, frustrations, and resentment to the point where these differences seem insurmountable. But in many instances, the culture clashes might have been avoidable. If the mergers and acquisition leaders had only bothered to facilitate better communication, bringing different sides to the table, to openly hash out the issues, many more mergers might well have been successful.

"Founding Frenemies"[2]

Think the forging of our nation's Constitution was free of conflict? Think again. Two of its leading proponents, John Adams and Thomas Jefferson, became bitter rivals. Both men were brilliant and heroic in their own ways, but they had such fundamental differences that they reached a point of hating each other's guts, and that animosity made almost every sentence of that blessed parchment a bone of contention. Put simply, Adams was a Federalist who felt the new United States should be more centralized to strengthen and maintain the union, while Jefferson wanted to limit federal powers to prevent another monarchy. The bitter division led to some nasty name-calling. At one point, during the 1800 election, Jefferson called Adams a "hideous hermaphroditical character." Someone on Adams's side, maybe Adams himself, called Jefferson a "mean-spirited, low-lived fellow." Yet they somehow bridged the animosity, leaning into their conflict to produce one of the greatest documents in the history of mankind, including the Bill of Rights, which was added on after much lobbying from Jefferson and James Monroe. It's my belief that, without that conflict, the Constitution would not have had the balance and nuance that makes its list of laws and rights so eternal. Diversity of thought, and a willingness to keep fighting, made this living document something for all mankind. Evidently, Jefferson and Adams thought so too. A dozen years after their rift, Adams wrote to Jefferson. "You and I ought not to die, before We have explained ourselves to each other." They kept corresponding until they died, within hours of each other, on July 4, 1826, exactly fifty years after Independence Day.

The smallest of misunderstandings can lead to complete dysfunction within a workforce. When I worked as a consultant to the Holiday Inn in the late 1980s, soon after the hotel chain had been acquired by the British consumer conglomerate Bass, morale stunk. Then based in Atlanta, the US staff was given a list of instructions on how to behave around visiting British executives: always where a white shirt, only lace-up shoes, no loafers . . . Can you imagine coming into the country and headquarters of the company you just acquired and demanding that your local employees change the way they dress? Not only was it insulting, it was a weird form of cultural imperialism. As a result, the various teams struggled to integrate, much less communicate. That particular merger was rocky for almost a decade before the Holiday Inn started turning a profit again.

Now imagine the challenge of merging Eastern and Western cultures, where the norms can be so far apart that they can't even find a consensus on the color of the sky. I got a taste of this level of disconnect when I was working for the Asia Pacific division of Sheraton, which put me through an Asian management training course. I learned that Japanese culture tends to be more risk-averse and that individuals prefer not to be too assertive. They often smile out of embarrassment, and it pains them to give someone negative feedback or tell them no.

As a vocally assertive and straight-shooting American, I could have walked into a disaster, never knowing where I stood or how I might be offending my counterparts. But, in my newfound awareness, I was able to adjust my approach, even bowing slightly when speaking with someone because I understood the importance of these outward signs of respect. These gestures may seem small, but failure to recognize and act upon these cultural differences could have built up a level of resistance that would have made it impossible for my suggestions to be heard in the way they were intended. Far from being able to facilitate any tough conversations, they'd have run for the hills at the sight of me.

East Meets West

Yolanda Conyers, whom you met in chapter 7, "Listen to Win," is all too familiar with the challenges of being that bridge. She played a key role in helping to bring together the legacy cultures of both the Lenovo and the IBM personnel. Many remaining employees from both iconic companies bristled at the idea of the takeover and were resistant to change. Lenovo's Chinese leaders had been extending themselves, learning English and conducting meetings in their second language, and immersing themselves in US culture. Members of the global leadership team did exchanges, working out of IBM's White Plains, New York, headquarters, pushing themselves way out of their comfort zones. But there was still plenty of conflict to resolve.

Among the major differences Yolanda quickly grasped was her Chinese colleagues' reluctance to speak up in meetings. It wasn't that they didn't have strong opinions so much as the fact that public disagreement was considered immensely disrespectful. In Chinese culture, *miànzi*, or "face," loosely refers to a concept of respect, honor, and social standing, and actions that are deemed disrespectful can cause someone to "lose face." Once that happens, resentment will get in the way of healthy conflict. To prevent this from happening, Yolanda employed a few simple techniques to help the legacy Lenovo associates speak up without fear of causing offense.

First, she would scan the conference room, looking for telltale signs of concern from a few of the meeting participants whose silence had been the most deafening, like a furrowed brow, folded arms, or averted eyes. Then she made a point of calling on an individual in an encouraging way.

"Alice," she might say, referring to this hypothetical Chinese colleague's English name. "We'd really value your expertise on this topic. Please will you share your opinion about relocating such and such manufacturing operations to Guangzhou? Do you agree, or do you foresee any difficulties?" (Again, this is hypothetical.)

Inviting Alice to express herself in this way took some of the pressure off.

"In school, mainland children are taught to be humble and told it's arrogant to go first in a conversation," Yolanda explained to me. "You never want to appear like a know-it-all."

Alice could then speak up because she was being *asked* to do it, not because she *chose* to interject. She felt free to share what was really on her mind because of Yolanda's gentle invitation to do just that. Once Alice spoke up, the way was paved for others in the room to follow with their own concerns, resulting in an honest discussion about some of the potential pitfalls that her new IBM colleagues might never have known.

Narrowing the cultural divide was a years-long process of learning and dialogue at Lenovo. Nothing was too small to trigger a grievance or misunderstanding that could spiral out of control. Even inadvertently scheduling something during a national holiday that the Western or Eastern person doing the scheduling knew nothing about could cause offense. Western executives who relocated to Beijing had to learn chopstick etiquette and show a willingness to drink *baijiu*, a high-volume white liquor, to build camaraderie and trust with their local co-workers. Chinese colleagues who transferred to the merged company's new Raleigh, North Carolina, headquarters joined their American counterparts at local sports events and barbecues.

Everyone was trying, but it was a steep and ongoing climb to mutual understanding. Yolanda's special brand of sensitivity and diplomacy was needed at every major meeting around the globe from Italy to Brazil, to every major office in China and the rest of East Asia. She was the cultural referee who instigated the tough conversations and kept everyone engaged so that well-informed decision-making could take place with everyone on board.

"Leaders need to learn how to navigate across different cultures, whether that's from other parts of the country or other regions of the world," Yolanda told me. "If people don't take the time to seek out and understand different cultures, they end up talking past each other and missing out on crucial perspectives and input, and that is what diversity is all about."

That doesn't mean there will be no future conflict, or that cultural misunderstandings will never happen. But there are smart ways to initiate a dialogue no matter how challenging the circumstances. Yolanda and her team were able to devise a system for meetings where one person or group could no longer talk over the rest. They developed "East Meets West" training on how to communicate, manage conflict, and talk about their differences.

Everyone could have their say, creating opportunities for each person to speak and laying the foundation for tough yet productive conversations instead of the usual communication breakdowns. As a result, Lenovo made history as a global merger—the first between Eastern and Western cultures to truly succeed. The tech giant, which is now a Fortune Global 500 company, went on to acquire several other major computer and electronics firms, including Motorola and Japan's Fujitsu, and at the time of writing, was enjoying surging growth, with a staggering $60 billion in revenue.

Yolanda happily retired back to her Texas home with plenty of air miles for her next family vacation. With global leadership teams now well established to facilitate tough conversations across functions and cultures, her job as the bridge builder was done.

Taffer Toolkit Takeaways

1. *Keep it real.* Don't let them off the hook as you confront them in real time. Until your adversary can really hear you, that point of contention is always going to fester. Understand that, in many ways, forcing conflict is an act of love.

2. ***Don't apologize.*** Recognize that forcing an open and honest dialogue about the issues is good for everyone. Never say you're sorry for what you believe. Besides, constructive conflict is a means of getting both sides to a better place.

3. ***Gently does it.*** When you force someone to confront the truth, you can crack them open just wide enough that they can receive. But it needs to be done with the utmost care. Forcing the kind of engagement that heals requires plenty of compassion and emotional intelligence.

4. ***Present hard evidence.*** It's much harder for someone to run away from a truth that's written in black and white. Let the facts, or even a neutral third party, help you to utter some uncomfortable truths that can bring greater clarity, understanding, or closure.

5. ***Adjust to different communication styles,*** especially when the other side comes from a different culture. Failure to recognize and act upon these cultural differences could build up a level of resistance that makes it impossible for your arguments or suggestions to be heard in the way they were intended.

6. ***Pave the way.*** Initiate dialogue by making it easy for the other side to speak up. Notice from facial expressions and other body language if they have something to say, then coax it out of them in an encouraging way. Don't ever let them retreat from the dialogue. The whole point of being a bridge is to get everyone to the other side.

10

PREPARE FOR THE LONG HAUL

*You may have to fight many battles
before you win the war. Patience and
class are your keys to victory.*

Hong Kong business consultant Richard Suen had serious con-
nections. He knew officials inside the People's Republic of China
with the power to grant licensing concessions to casino's in
Macau, the former Portuguese enclave that is now an international
gambling hub known as the Vegas of the East. In 2001, long before
anyone else had an inkling, he'd heard that the Chinese government
was considering opening up gaming in that special administrative
region to American casinos. Richard shared this knowledge with a
friend who happened to be the brother of the late Sheldon Adelson,
owner of the Las Vegas Sands (LVS) Corporation. Mr. Adelson, like
any casino operator, was eager to gain a foothold in that untapped,
lucrative market, so he engaged Richard to arrange crucial meetings
to make it happen.

By 2002, Richard's introductions enabled LVS to obtain licensing
from the Chinese authorities allowing it to open its first casino—the
Sands Macau—inside this vibrant territory along the south coast of

China, across the Pearl River Delta from Hong Kong. In return, he was promised a $5 million "success fee" along with 2 percent of the earnings of the casino for the twenty-year duration of the license, which was set to expire in 2022. By then, the Sands was projected to have earned $17.1 billion in profits. Adelson earned his $265 million investment back within the year. But guess what: Richard got bupkis.

At first, he tried every avenue to get his due, including appealing to Adelson's better conscience. He had leveraged several important relationships that Adelson, as a Westerner, would have found impossible to create for himself, and spent more than a year of his time and energy as a middleman, smoothing the way for face-to-face meetings with senior members of the Chinese government. But there was no paper contract. The entire deal was founded on the Chinese concept of *guanxi*: a cherished code of honor, reciprocity, and commitment.

This system of social networking and influence goes way beyond networking as we understand it in the West. It's fundamental to the way business is conducted in that culture, where personal trust is the currency for any business dealings and can take years to establish. *Guanxi* is, above all, about mutual respect and doing right by each other. It's a principle Richard lives by. When Adelson thumbed his nose at it, scoffing that Richard's contributions were "useless," Richard could not let it go. Not only was the response an affront to Richard, it was an insult to his culture.

But time and again, Richard was told to forget about it. Give up. This was a David and Goliath battle that was impossible to win. Some warned him that the Nevada judges would not be favorable to an outsider, and that the legal system would close ranks to protect one of their own.

"Move on," people told him. "You'll never win against that guy. He is litigious as hell and will just keep throwing more money at this.

He'd rather go bankrupt himself than lose to you. Cut your losses now!"

Instead, Richard went shopping for a lawyer. A good one. He eventually found John O'Malley, whose firm had gone to battle with Adelson in the past. O'Malley told Richard he believed in him, and that he'd fight beside him for as long as it took.

Mental Toughness

I don't think either of them expected it would take fifteen years and three trials. The jury kept voting in favor of the plaintiff. Richard won each time, including a breach-of-contract ruling in 2008 that awarded him $44 million and, in 2013, after an LVS appeal that back-fired, $70 million. But the money was never paid. Adelson kept on appealing, going up through the court system in the hopes a friendly judge in the Nevada Supreme Court would see the evidence in a whole new way. It was looking like this case would cycle in and out of the court system through infinity.

During trial three, the judge upheld the previous decision in favor of Richard but reversed the previous award amount. His lawyers shook their heads at the unusual ruling. It was back to the drawing board. Under the terms of Richard's initial agreement with LVS, he would by now have been owed $346.9 million, including interest. The LVS legal team said not one penny more than $3.76 million. Then, mysteriously, on day two of the third trial, Adelson's lawyers relented. They settled for an undisclosed amount that likely landed somewhere in the mid-dle, with no more appeals. Richard and his lawyer had finally won.

I had to ask Richard if it was worth all those years of traveling back and forth between his home in Hong Kong and Las Vegas, more than seven thousand miles and fifteen time zones away.

"Not for one moment did I consider giving up," he told me. "This whole fifteen-year saga I never let bother me one bit. I had faith in my lawyers and faith in myself. I never doubted that we were standing up for what was right."

Admittedly, it was a far longer game than anyone could have imagined. Adelson's intractable position aside, the Las Vegas court system was inundated with backdated cases, so the entire process moved at a glacial pace. But Richard compartmentalized. When he wasn't in Vegas, he continued to run his business and live his life. And when he was in Vegas, spending weeks in a hotel room far from his family, outside the courtroom he distracted himself, catching shows, reading books, enjoying meals with his legal team, and driving through the desert to see sights like the Hoover Dam or take long walks in Red Rock Canyon.

He put everything into the fight when he had to but rested and recharged in between court dates. He never dwelled on his adversary, whom he regarded as "someone beneath my station" and not worthy of his emotional energy. Doing battle with the corporate bully was no different to him than getting up in the morning and doing his job.

"Mentally, I am tough. I did whatever was necessary to prepare for the depositions and trial, but, when that wasn't happening, I just put the whole thing in a box."

It helped that Richard never felt alone. By then, he had formed a close bond with O'Malley, who often stayed in Vegas over the weekends to keep his client-turned-friend company rather than return to Los Angeles to see his own family. After that last day in court, Richard couldn't decide who he was happier for: himself, or O'Malley, whose faith in his case had finally paid off.

"The settlement wasn't the full amount we deserved, but it was substantial, and the moment we wrapped up that last case, John and

I drove back to LA, where he turned in his papers and retired. It felt so good that he could end his career on such a high note. It was complete vindication."

The patience demonstrated by Richard and his legal team is uncommon. When most of us engage in conflict, we want to see a resolution—a win—then and there. But that's not always realistic. Some of the greatest victories require playing the long game with tenacity. Engagement with your adversary might happen in stages, and take weeks, months, or years. If you've already made the calculation and decided it's worth the fight, it's probably also worth the wait.

Just remember to manage your expectations. In the extended conflict, you can't expect the satisfaction of an apology or total capitulation to your point of view in the heat of the moment. The immediate resolution—the win or draw—may not be forthcoming. So use that downtime to your advantage. Plan out your attack and think about the larger goal. And because this is the kind of conflict that stretches out over time, preserve your energy. Don't burn yourself out right at the beginning. Sure, there will be those intense moments—even yelling where necessary. But mostly your engagement will just simmer as you plot out that next step, and the next. Meanwhile, like Richard, you've got to treat the long-term engagement like your job, or your mission.

Of course, I realize we don't all have access to a crack legal team willing to work pro bono, although if you are up against a huge corporation and have done your homework, it's certainly possible to find an advocate. There's also nothing stopping you from being your own best champion as you calmly gather your facts to build a case that can eventually bring down the bully, whether that's a boss, a company, a bureaucrat, or a school board. And, as you stand up for your righteous cause, you may gradually notice that others are willing to stand up beside you.

One Scathing Screed

Consider what happened across the country between 2020 and 2021, when parents came out of extended pandemic lockdowns as their children attempted to take their classes remotely. One by one, they became aware of some education practices that they felt were detrimental to the physical and mental well-being of their children. These parents, as well as many educators, rose up to speak their minds, whether the issues were prolonged school closures or teaching six-year-old children about sex and gender issues or critical race theory. For the first time, as children interacted with their teachers via Zoom on their laptops, parents could see what was being taught, and many objected.

New York City father Andrew Gutmann wasn't the first parent across the country to protest, but he was something of a unicorn because of his willingness to speak up and his ability to forcefully express himself. His approach caught the nation's attention. Parents kept mostly silent because they feared the derision of others in their community and did not want to risk backlash toward their children for speaking views that others might not like. Then Gutmann, whose daughter attended the $54,000-a-year private Brearley School, wrote scathing screed against "antiracism initiatives" that he believed were trying to make her feel guilty about her skin color. That 1,700-word letter, initially just intended to be read by the other Brearley parents and school community members, went viral and started a movement.

Most parents of means would kill to get their kid in a school like Brearley. The competition is fierce because it's considered a pathway to an Ivy League college and a bright future for their offspring, not to mention a certain social standing among their parents. But the Gutmann family, with the full support of their daughter, made the tough choice to not reenroll her after seven years of the school because "we no longer have confidence that our daughter will receive the quality of education necessary to further her development into a critically thinking, responsible, enlightened, and civic minded adult."

It was a long missive that covered a lot of ground about the issues of the day, concluding, "that Brearley has begun to teach what to think, instead of how to think. I object that the school is now fostering an environment where our daughters, and our daughters' teachers, are afraid to speak their minds in class for fear of 'consequences.'"

In subsequent news interviews, Gutmann explained that his protest letter was the result of many conversations with other Brearley parents, and parents at similar private schools. Through these discussions, he came to learn that many of his fellow parents felt exactly as he did, regardless of their political affiliations. But they feared the consequences of giving voice to their objections.

Then something interesting happened. After Gutmann's letter circulated, more frustrated parents rose up. An anonymous group with kids attending the city's most elite private schools, including Dalton, Brearley, and Trinity, funded billboards on trucks parked outside these institutions with slogans like *Diversity Not Indoctrination*, and *Teach* How *to Think, Not* What *to Think*, and *Woke School? Speak Out.*

Whatever your thoughts on the state of education in America, it was an effective grassroots campaign that turned into a national movement. Parents all over the country started showing up at school board meetings delivering fiery speeches on behalf of their kids. In Virginia, the chorus of parents from all walks of life, political persuasions, ethnicities, and identities cried out against similar practices. In Fairfax County, at the public school board meeting, a military veteran named Zia Tompkins had plenty to say:

"This kind of stuff is poison. This will tear this country apart if it becomes a part of our fabric. How do I know this? I just came from the Middle East, where people sort themselves by ethnicity, by religion, by race, and these areas are ungovernable. If you sink this into our kids, if you divide our kids up and have them see only race, creed, culture, religion, you will be destroying this country. Believe me. I have seen it. I have lived it."

At Loudoun County in Virginia, a school board meeting made national news as parents and teachers decried what was happening in *their* schools. State by state, from New Jersey, to Maine, to Florida, to Oregon, this outspokenness at school board meetings spread as parents watched each other on social media and the news and found their own voices.

The pushback over how children were being taught caught fire because these issues directly affected those who we, as humans, care about most. Thousands of moms and dads were galvanized, coming to the conclusion that silence was no longer an option. Wherever you stand on the topics highlighted by Gutmann and other parents across the country, their strategy—creating websites and campaigns, writing letters to the editor in papers of record, investing in billboards, and showing up and speaking up en masse at local school board meetings across the country—were extremely effective methods for creating a groundswell.

Family Affair

It took months for the message to marinate and embolden these concerned parents and may well take at least another school year and election cycle for them to see the results of their courage, but these parents have been heard, by the whole country, and slowly the education policies will begin to shift. Like one of those huge cruise ships that look like floating building blocks, something that big takes a while to turn.

And the same goes for family conflict. When tension affects a group of loved ones living in close quarters, the need for patience and persistence is never greater. These are folks you must live with for the rest of your life, so it can often behoove you to take it slow. They're not going anywhere, and neither are you.

Rachel grew up Jewish in New Jersey, yet she fell in love with a man whose folks were born-again Christians from rural Georgia. That was all very well in the beginning of the marriage. Rachel enjoyed the family customs, like Easter Egg hunts and decorating the tree on Christmas Eve. But when Rachel and her husband decided to move to his hometown during COVID, shortly after their first child was born, she started feeling the culture clash.

Within this large Bible Belt family, Rachel's mother-in-law is the matriarch. Rachel loves and admires the woman, but conflict became unavoidable when her mother-in-law started suggesting that she raise her son in the church. The mother-in-law started a campaign to convert Rachel, quoting scripture and leaving Bibles and crosses everywhere. Because they come from different faiths, Rachel and her husband had made the conscious decision not to raise their children in either religion, giving them the support and space they'd need to make their own choices when they were old enough. So the mother-in-law is overstepping—a problem that is going to have to be addressed before the child is old enough to understand and be influenced by his grandmother's Bible bedtime stories.

It's a real dilemma. Rachel's mother-in-law rates a ten on the conflict calculator. She's extremely important in Rachel's life and not someone she can walk away from in an entire extended family where she is the outsider. Yet Rachel is determined to raise her son in the way she believes is best for him. That is nonnegotiable. Meanwhile, the tension has been slowly growing, like a cancer. It's gotten to the point where Rachel won't let her mother-in-law babysit. She's putting some safe distance between them, even though her mother-in-law lives less than a five-minute drive away. While Rachel has her husband's full support, she knows a tough conversation is coming.

I've been encouraging Rachel not to put it off any longer. If she doesn't deal with the conflict it could ruin her family. She needs to get into her car, drive over to her mother-in-law's house, sit down with her, and tell her how she really feels. Their common ground is obvious. The two women both dearly love that baby boy and want what's best for him. That's where they need to start. But the conflict won't be resolved within that single conversation. There will be several uncomfortable moments. These generational and cultural differences run deep and can't be bridged overnight. But over weeks or months, through transparency, compassion, and trust, Rachel can make this work. Through a deliberate step-by-step process, she can help her mother-in-law to accept some boundaries that will ultimately ensure she remains a huge part of her grandson's life. Time is on their side.

Be Gracious in Victory

To recap, long-haul conflict can be a powerful tool in winning your case, effecting meaningful society change, or simply handling a family dynamic that allows everyone to live with each other in harmony. Achieving these goals can take more time than you know, and they are worthy of the investment. But you also need to know when the conflict is over. There is nothing to be gained from continuing to litigate when you've already landed your point.

Plush was an Italian bar/restaurant in the suburbs of Philadelphia that was owned by a divorced couple. The business ran successfully until the divorce. Bruno and Shari worked beautifully together. Then he cheated on her. Shari divorced him after finding out about the infidelity, and their small town knew the entire story. Shari was beloved by the community. Customers stayed away and refused to support the husband's business because it was now viewed as "against" the wife because she wasn't showing up to work. Bruno was the business's chef and Shari ran the front of the house. Without Shari's contribution to the business, operations unraveled, and the business began to fail. Complicating the issue was the couple's young daughter, who was caught in the middle.

For the business to work, I had to break the unresolved conflict and resentment between husband and wife (I often find myself in the position of relationship counselor, go figure). On my second day, I managed to convince Shari to come back to work without her husband's knowledge. When Bruno saw her, he grew noticeably uncomfortable. He felt challenged. But by forcing them to work together, they had no choice but to address their feelings of hurt and disappointment head-on, exposing the real conflict between them.

I pushed hard. I confronted the husband about his behavior, and I confronted the wife about taking her hurt out on their business, allowing it to fail. I confronted them both about the impact on their daughter. Getting all the feelings out in the open helped the woman's willingness to come back to work. The customers followed. Both Bruno and Shari stepped up and began working together again. The ex-husband and wife will likely never remarry, but they have cleared the air, and now have a working relationship.

As the conflict played out, I could feel the mood shift. It was obvious. Both halves of the couple suddenly realized how their behavior and attitude toward each other was affecting their business and their family. At that point there was nothing more to be said. My job was done, and Bruno and Shari understood it was time to move forward.

Constructive conflict saved the day. But once the beef was over, it was over. Extending the argument or relitigating the past would have only served to set them back once more.

It's crucial to understand when to shut up. I've witnessed too many individuals make their case then lose their audience because they just couldn't stop talking. Recognize when you've won and then gracefully exit or change the subject.

Again, this is about maintaining the respect and dignity of your opponent, which should be the through line of any constructive conflict. With the facts in your possession, and your emotions in check, you are prepared for conflict. Although it may seem counterintuitive, coming at your adversary from a position of respect and dignity through the beginning, middle, and end of the engagement is what makes you the real winner.

Six Signs of Victory

So how will you know you've won the argument, and how long will you have to wait for a change in behavior, attitudes, or opinions? Here are some clues to look for:

1. Your opponent begins engaging with you more constructively.
2. The subject changes and the conversation flows in another, more conciliatory direction.
3. There's been a pause where you can tell from eye contact and facial expression that the other party is really listening to you and digesting the points you've made.
4. They ask follow-up questions that demonstrate a genuine desire to understand what you mean, and how they can do better in the future.
5. The volume and defenses go down.
6. You hug it out!

Yours is not the only point of view. Let your adversary know you have respect despite your differences. Your purpose is not to change those with whom you are in conflict, just their point of view. Too often we find ourselves thinking that if we change our minds, we lose our dignity or the other person's respect. That feeling will likely cause us to dig into our position and keep the conflict going. Allowing the other parties to keep their dignity intact as you attempt to change their minds opens the door to a positive result with minimal cost. Just remember. *No* victory laps!

But, again, it doesn't always happen right away. You must give your adversaries some space to mull it over and lick their wounds. I've had intense debates with friends with whom I've disagreed about politics. It gets loud, but it's an enjoyable discourse between people who have a love and respect for each other. My opponent will disagree with me down to the last second. They'll never concede a point. But I've noticed when we're speaking a few days later that they've modified their opinions. They'll never admit it to my face or say it in writing, but I'll take it!

For more complicated issues beyond some friendly dinner table banter, the effort is ongoing. It has taken weeks or months for me to see the evidence of a change in mindset. Some folks are too stubborn and proud. It can take patience to see positive and lasting results from constructive conflict. Meanwhile, it costs you nothing to be gracious in victory.

Chances are this isn't your first conflict, nor will it be your last, so be that person who fights fair and has the reputation for being straight-shooting, well intentioned, and compassionate. Take pleasure that your facts have prevailed, and that you can move forward in a conflict-free environment but maintain your respect of your (former) opponent. Never, ever kick them while they're down!

Taffer Toolkit Takeaways

1. **Take it slow and smart.** Engagement with your adversary might happen in stages and take weeks, months, or years. But that's okay. If it's worth the fight, it's probably also worth the wait.

2. **Practice mental toughness.** Don't let the fight drain your energy. Rest and recharge between engagements. Prepare, but also try to compartmentalize. Don't dwell on your adversary; save it for the court date or the face-to-face interaction.

3. **Manage your expectations.** In the extended conflict, you can't expect the satisfaction of an apology or total capitulation to your point of view in the heat of the moment. The immediate resolution—the win or draw—may not be forthcoming.

4. **Use downtime to your advantage.** Plan out your attack and think about the larger goal. There's also nothing stopping you from being your own best champion as you calmly gather your facts to build a case that can eventually bring down the bully.

5. **Find an advocate, or others who will stand beside you in your fight.** Time, patience, and smart strategizing will bring others along with you.

6. **Leverage time in a family conflict.** When tension affects a group of loved ones living in close quarters, the need for patience and persistence is never greater.

7. **Be gracious in victory.** As long and drawn-out as this battle may have been, you need to know when the conflict is over.

8. **Do not risk losing by over-litigating your point.** Recognize when you've won, or at least accept the draw, then gracefully make your exit. And no victory laps!

THE EVOLUTION OF A CONFLICT CHAMPION

We can all grow in our conflict skills. As we mature as leaders of ourselves, our businesses, our communities, and our families, we can all take these tools for constructive engagement to right wrongs, heal relationships, change minds, and stand up for our principles. Like any life skill, this is a muscle we can build through practice, refining and strengthening our adversarial chops with every interaction. With that in mind, let me leave you with one last story.

Miko Branch, the founder and owner of global hair care company Miss Jessie's, has always been feisty. Miko had to defend herself against the schoolyard bullies of the middle school she attended in Queens, New York, where physical assaults were not out of the ordinary. When she was bussed to a school in a wealthier neighborhood, she had to face down the mean girls with their sharp tongues and snide remarks. As a young woman in her late teens, when she cleaned homes for the family business and marketed these services for her domineering father, she found the confidence and resilience to push back against some bad decisions. As an expectant single mother running a beauty salon in Brooklyn, Miko stood up for herself against a greedy landlord, slick suppliers, and more than a few unruly customers.

"We're all born with spirit, and mine just kind of moves in that way," Miko told me. "If something bothers my whole being, if I feel violated, be it a conversation or an interception that stops me from moving forward, I tend to really feel it, so conflict is not something I can run away from."

Miko is soft-spoken with a gentle and gracious demeanor. She gives people chances, listening and asking questions to get to the bottom of a situation that feels off to her. She is not one to jump to conclusions or overreact in the moment. So you wouldn't necessarily expect the fierceness that came out when someone threatened her ability to earn a living and feed and clothe her baby boy, for example. Or when buyers at a retail chain tried to strong-arm her into accepting payment terms that would have hurt the cash flow of her growing hair-care product business. But when the evidence mounts that someone is trying to take advantage, Miko's steely resolve comes through, and her opposition rarely makes the same mistake twice.

But her conflict style has evolved over the years. She's "a different Miko" from the young woman who had to assert herself in the competitive world of hairdressing school on Thirty-Fourth Street in Manhattan, "where one girl got jumped and had her hair weave pulled out because they thought she looked like Naomi Campbell." Today, Miko leverages her conflict skills in more nuanced ways both as the face of her company and internally at Miss Jessie's, where she leads a team of about a dozen professionals and associates.

"We New Yorkers tend to be more direct and to the point, but now there's more layering to my approach."

Miko intentionally adjusts her tone and chooses her words according to the circumstance, the person, and the broader goal of the interaction. She tackles conflict from what she describes as "the front end," deciding first what is to be gained either personally or professionally from a confrontation and whether it's worth the fallout (the conflict calculator).

"My mind goes to what I want the outcome to be, and I work my way backward from there. If it's a friend or family member, my interaction is in line with that. If I don't care if I ever see you again, my approach adjusts accordingly. But if I learn something during the interaction that causes me to change my position, I'll acknowledge it and stay open to resolving something a totally different way."

She's become more strategic about where she wants to go, and how far she needs to push her point to get there. She fire-tests her own position, questioning her own assumptions before bringing the fight to her opponent. She comes at it from a position of respect and fairness, giving her adversary a chance to explain or convince her otherwise (the rules of engagement). And she pays attention to the words and reactions of the person on the other end of the engagement, listening not just to win the argument but to ascertain whether her point is landing in the way she intended (the engagement meter).

"My reaction is more measured and there is a lot more three-dimensional thinking going on," Miko explained. "A few years ago, whatever was on my mind was going to come out and I didn't think about the consequence. But now I ask myself if there is going to be a repercussion to the relationship or the situation and do I care?"

More often these days, Miko will choose to be diplomatic and move on (pick your battles). But that wasn't an option when she found herself being undermined by a new hire. She hoped that this senior-level finance person would take over a lot of the day-to-day operational and financial oversight, to free up her time. But whenever she discussed a strategy with him, he'd "yes" her, and then go off and do just the opposite, including giving the wrong direction to an external partner that would lead to an increased and unnecessary expense to the business.

Again, Miko didn't react in the moment. She ate the cost and let it slide. "He was new, and it takes some people some time to warm up, so I didn't want to rattle him."

But, in week three of his new job, he did it again, and her business got another surprise bill. Miko didn't want to make assumptions as to why her new hire did this, so she calmly asked him why, then explained why these sudden pivots wouldn't work for her.

"Our relationship is important to me," she told him. "If we agree we are going to do something, and you deviate from the plan, it complicates things and makes me uncomfortable."

He wrote back and apologized, but there have been a few more red flags since and Miko senses he's annoyed. "I think there might be a ripple in the seam, but time will tell." (Prepare for the long haul.)

She made herself clear about her needs and expectations of this employee, "because I don't like to let things fester," but she chose not to start off hot. As a boss, she's also more careful about giving the people who report to her "a sense of being on a level playing field in terms of dignity and respect." She's also willing to play the long game and give him the opportunity to correct course.

But by no means is Miko's conflict strategy always so restrained. When I say she uses all the tools in my Taffer Toolkit, I mean *all*.

For one thing, she pays attention to the location where a conflict takes place, making a point to speak with her employees in a way that does not intimidate. She subtly creates a more neutral and casual environment, "even though they are well aware that I am their supervisor." For her, a neutral location can include:

Seated side by side with her employee in her office, versus perched behind a desk like a boss.

In an off-site location, like a coffee shop.

A stroll around the office neighborhood.

"I never want someone who works for me to feel under attack. The right physical setting helps create an informal tone and lets them know we can have a more open, honest dialogue," Miko explains. "If I can put someone at ease in terms of the physical setting as I let them share in my process, it's just a conversation between two people, and maybe I can discover something new along the way."

She also puts a lot of emphasis on the positive. Christmas bonus time is the one thing that gives her joy as a leader. Writing those checks to reward her staff for all their hard work over the previous year feels incredibly gratifying.

"I probably get more excited about handing out these checks than my team is about receiving them."

As a small business leader, these payments were entirely discretionary and well above the industry standard. But one of Miko's employees was less than grateful. He'd been phoning it in all year, so his bonus, while generous, wasn't as high as some of his co-workers'—a fact he was aware of, as he happened to run the payroll department, so he decided to approach Miko and ask for more.

"Get the hell out of my office *now*!" she screamed at him at the top of her lungs as he scurried back to his desk. (To yell or not to yell.)

It got so loud that the rest of her team came running to see what had happened. Miko fired the man a few months later, after catching him in a lie.

"Don't let me fool you. Sometimes you've just got to keep it real. I may have matured, but the old Miko still comes out when necessary."

From Minor to Major League

Still don't feel quite ready to step into the ring with an adversary? Any kind of confrontation can be intimidating for a lot of people, so how about this? Create a minor conflict in a safe setting, with your spouse, for example.

Think about some minor thing that your partner does that's been slightly irritating to you for years. Maybe you never felt it was worth bringing up. You love this person, and all his great qualities, so much that you let it slide each time your husband leaves his socks on the bedroom floor. Bring it up, keeping in mind the setting and rules of engagement, and give the *Taffer Toolkit for Conflict* a road test.

"Now, honey, about those socks . . . ?"

Next, put this book down for a week and be on the lookout for another situation where constructive engagement could make your life better. Maybe your neighbor takes days to pick up her recycling bin from the end of the driveway. In addition to being unsightly and annoying every time you look out your kitchen window, the giant blue bin rattles in the wind and drifts over to the end of your front yard. There is absolutely no reason why politely asking that she put away the bin in a timely manner should turn into a showdown. But if it does, you know you have the tools in your back pocket.

After a few more of these honest engagements, some heated, some not, you should be feeling more confident. A major-league conflict could involve something as high stakes as the custody of your kids or a confrontation with a work colleague doing something unethical. It could be a political disagreement with a group of people demonstrating over an issue, or an encounter with a mob of noisy "protesters" who are trying to coerce you into kneeling in the street. Maybe you don't feel like making a power fist while trying to eat at a street café as an obnoxious kid screams in your face. Or maybe it's a critical matter of making your case to the local authorities to keep your small business open so that you and your employees can feed your families. You can and should stand up for yourself. If not now, when?

You're more than ready.

Your Constructive Conflict Checklist

Before you step into the arena, ask yourself:

1) Have I completed a cost-benefit analysis?

- Make sure the prize is worth it. Trivial matters may not be the best use of your time and effort.

- Calculate all of the costs—personal, professional, emotional, and financial.

- Make sure you are prepared to lose. Many risks are worth taking. Some are not.

- Don't be afraid to walk away—if that's what your analysis shows.

2) Are your emotions in control?

- Approach the conflict calmly. The best way to do this is to have done your homework.

- It's okay to show emotion when you engage—just be sure you are in charge. Keep your comments based on your facts.

- It's okay to express how you feel—but don't presume to speak for your opponents about their feelings.

Once inside the arena, ask yourself:

3) Am I treating opponents with respect and allowing them to maintain their dignity?

- Use proper forms of address—no name-calling, no belittling nicknames.

- Maintain your own dignity—no eye-rolling, sniggering, or other body language cues that convey disrespect.

- Listen to what the other person is saying—and check with them to make sure you understand their meaning.

- Survey to see if the setting is appropriate and not one in which you or your opponent feel uncomfortable, embarrassed, or otherwise compromised.

4) Are you making an effort to find common ground with your opponents?

- Offer examples of where you and your opponent agree to establish common ground but also to limit the boundaries of the conflict.
- Share specific examples that pinpoint the nature of the conflict so that your opponent can see "where you're coming from."
- Share, if appropriate, similar personal anecdotes that help establish a shared experience between the two of you.

5) Am I focused on presenting my arguments with the most relevant facts and compelling evidence?

- Skip the complaints. Complaining doesn't change minds or win arguments.
- Review your facts. Make sure they are accurate, supportive of your argument, and easy to understand. Have examples to show how the facts apply to the situation.
- Show how your idea or solution is preferable. Use real evidence and examples—not what-ifs.

6) Am I giving myself the respect I deserve?

- Do not feel you must be apologetic about holding a point of view or offering a particular solution. You are entitled to your ideas.

Make sure *you* are sure—review your facts and evidence, and if you think they're not strong enough, go back and do more homework. If you are sure, then present them with confidence and no apology.

ACKNOWLEDGMENTS

To my wife, Nicole, thank you for always being my sounding board—twenty-five years, millions of miles, and thousands of days on the road.

And to Sean Walker and the rest of Team Taffer, you know who you are. Thank you for always stepping up to turn my ideas/goals/visions into reality, including this book. Your support allowed me to take time to write something that makes me truly proud.

This book is rich in diverse detail and insights thanks to the individuals, identified and unidentified, who were generous enough to share their stories with me. To all of you, I am filled with gratitude.

Finally, to my literary team:

My agent, Byrd Leavell, thank you for believing in me and providing the sharpest feedback! My editors, Lisa Sharkey and Matt Harper, you opened my mind and made this book's message better. And my "book whisperer" Samantha Marshall. Sam, you heard me!

NOTES

1 THE CASE FOR CONFLICT

1. Valentine Lebedev, *Diary of a Cosmonaut: 211 Days in Space* (New York: Bantam Books, 1990).

2. Ibid, 139.

3. Ibid, 224–225.

4. Ibid, 284.

5. Ibid, 18.

6. Jerry Hirsch, "Mary Barra New CEO at GM, Most Powerful Female Exec in America [Q&A]," *Los Angeles Times*, December 11, 2013, https://www.latimes.com/business/autos/la-fi-hy-mary-barra-gm-ceo -20131211-story.html#axzz2rAIzEROr.

7. Jeff Weiss and Jonathan Hughes, "Want Collaboration?: Accept—and Actively Manage—Conflict," *Harvard Business Review*, March 2005, https://hbr.org/2005/03/want-collaboration-accept-and-actively -manage-conflict.

8. John P. Kotter, "The Good Fight: How Conflict Can Help Your Idea," *Harvard Business Review*, December 14, 2010, https://hbr.org/2010/12 /the-good-fight-how-conflict-ca.html#:~:text=To%20make%20 positive%2C%20lasting%20change,John%20P.

9. Ian K. Smith M.D., *Mind over Weight: Curb Cravings, Find Motivation, and Hit Your Number in 7 Simple Steps* (New York: St. Martin's Press, 2020).

10. A. Fowler, E. Field, and J. Mcmohan, "The Upside Of Conflict," *Stanford Social Innovation Review*, https://learn.twu.ca/pluginfile.php/171693 /mod_resource/content/1/The%20Upside%20of%20Conflict.pdf.

2   THE FIGHT IN MY HEAD

1.   Tzeses, Jennifer, "Tell Me Everything I Need to Know About Cognitive Dissonance," PSYCOM.com (undated), https://www.psycom.net /cognitive-dissonance.

4   THE RULES OF ENGAGEMENT

1.   United States Courts, "Setting Ground Rules - Civil Discourse and Difficult Decisions," https://www.uscourts.gov/educational-resources /educational-activities/setting-ground-rules-civil-discourse-and -difficult.

2.   Kate Taylor, "Starbucks has become a target of Trump-loving conservatives—and that's great news for the brand," *Business Insider*, February 5, 2017, https://www.businessinsider.com/why-trump -supporters-boycott-starbucks-2017-2.

3.   Sandy Grady, "A Bit of Blarney at Ron-Tip Love Feast," *Philadelphia Daily News/Orlando Sentinel*, March 19, 1986, https://www .orlandosentinel.com/news/os-xpm-1986-03-19-0210030090-story.html.

4.   Dartmouth PATH Review, https://onemindpsyberguide.org/apps /dartmouth-path/.

6   TO YELL OR NOT TO YELL

1.   Jon Taffer, *Raise the Bar: An Action-Based Method for Maximum Customer Reactions* (Seattle: Amazon Publishing, 2013).

7   LISTEN TO WIN

1.   Gina Qiao and Yolanda Conyers, *The Lenovo Way: Managing a Diverse Global Company for Optimal Performance* (New York: McGraw-Hill, 2014).

8   MEET ME ON THE CORNER

1.   David Shepardson, "Unfriendly skies: 2,500 unruly U.S. airline passengers reported in 2021," *Reuters*, May 24, 2021, https://www

.reuters.com/world/us/us-has-received-2500-unruly-airline-passenger
-reports-since-jan-1-2021-05-24/.

2. Theodore Kinni, "The Disney Brothers' Dilemma," *Family Business Magazine*, Spring 2004, https://www.familybusinessmagazine.com /disney-brothers-dilemma-0.

3. IDMb, "Snow White and the Seven Dwarfs" Trivia, https://m.imdb .com/title/tt0029583/trivia?tab=gf&ref_=tt_trv_gf.

4. Kinni, "The Disney Brothers' Dilemma."

5. Kinni, "The Disney Brothers' Dilemma."

6. Kinni, "The Disney Brothers' Dilemma."

7. "Jon Taffer of Bar Rescue Makes the Worst Manhattan – Meredith Vieira Show," https://www.reddit.com/r/cocktails/comments/4h0kyc /jon_taffer_of_bar_rescue_makes_the_worst/.

9 BE THE BRIDGE

1. Graham Kenny, "Don't Make This Common M&A Mistake," *Harvard Business Review*, March 16, 2020, https://hbr.org/2020/03/dont-make -this-common-ma-mistake.

2. Sarah Pruitt, "Jefferson & Adams: Founding Frenemies," The History Channel website, https://www.history.com/news/jefferson-adams -founding-frenemies.

ABOUT THE AUTHOR

Most people know Jon Taffer as a larger-than-life television personality who takes a no-holds-barred approach to helping hotels, restaurants, bars, and businesses reach their full potential. He is also an international celebrity, a *New York Times*–bestselling author, a highly sought-after hospitality and general business consultant, and the creator, executive producer, and star of one of Paramount Network's top shows, *Bar Rescue*. For nearly four decades, Jon has been at the forefront of the business management industry, offering his expertise to hundreds of thousands of properties and Fortune 500 companies, creating what industry experts called "the greatest nightclub in the world," and changing the game of football for its fans forever with the creation of football's Sunday Ticket.

As the creator, host, and executive producer of *Bar Rescue* on the Paramount Network, which just wrapped its eighth season, Jon has led the show to account for nearly 25 percent of the network's programing and over 90 million viewers. *Bar Rescue* spotlights Jon as he saves failing bars from looming closure, leveraging his four decades of unprecedented industry experience and trademarked "reaction management" strategy to offer advice on everything from menu design to cost management. In 2021 the show reached 223 episodes.

In the spring of 2019, Jon launched Taffer's Mixologist, a line of cocktail mixes that brings the craft experience to the home. Jon also partnered with Fransmart, the industry-leading franchise development company (the Halal Guys, Five Guys Burgers and Fries, QDOBA Mexican Grill), to create Taffer's Tavern, an innovative restaurant concept based on the Taffer's Safe Dining System™, creating one of the safest franchise brands in history. The first of many locations opened in Alpharetta, Georgia in November 2020.

As an author, Jon wrote *Don't Bullsh*t Yourself!*, a no-nonsense guide that helps people understand and overcome the excuses holding them back from success, and which became a *New York Times*, *Los Angeles Times*, and *Wall Street Journal* bestseller in its first week of release. Jon's first book, *Raise the Bar: An Action-Based Method for Maximum Customer Reactions*, also hit the *Wall Street Journal*'s bestseller list.

In 2018, Jon launched *The Jon Taffer Podcast*. The weekly show features his trademark straight talk and unapologetic approach to daily topics, current events, and celebrity interviews. Since its launch, Jon has interviewed celebrities and industry trailblazers such as Mark Cuban, Daymond John, Dr. Phil McGraw, Maria Menounos, Martellus Bennett, Jenny McCarthy, Jim Harbaugh, Dennis Miller, Barstool Sports Big Cat, Robert Irvine, Daniel Negreanu, Guy Fieri, Rick Harrison, and more.

As an entrepreneur and business expert, Jon has been featured in leading publications such as *Forbes* magazine, *Entrepreneur*, *Rolling Stone*, and the *New York Times*, among other prominent media outlets. He has appeared as a guest on shows ranging from *Rachael Ray* to *Jimmy Kimmel Live!* to *Good Morning America*. In addition, Jon is a regular guest on Fox Business Network, MSNBC, and CNBC.

Some of his past awards and accolades include:

- Visionary Leader Award
- Creator of the NFL's Sunday Ticket

- Nightclub Hall of Fame inductee
- United Kingdom's "Pub Master" distinction
- Dom Perignon Award of Excellence from UNLV's College of Hotel Administration
- The Friday's "Propeller Award" for the greatest contribution to their business

When he's not dedicating his time to bringing back businesses from the brink, Taffer volunteers with the Keep Memory Alive board of directors, supporting the mission of the Cleveland Clinic Lou Ruvo Center for Brain Health. He also regularly offers up his seasoned hospitality skills to the William F. Harrah College of Hotel Administration at the University of Nevada, Las Vegas, where he helps faculty develop curriculum that is in line with industry expectations and trends.

Married for over twenty years to his wife, Nicole, who he fell in love with at first sight at Super Bowl XXX, Jon spends what little spare time he has traveling with her. He also enjoys spending time with his daughter and grandson, and occasionally sipping one of his favorite cocktails: the godfather.